Treating the
Borderline Family
A Systemic Approach

Family Therapy
Theory, Practice, and Technique

Vincent D. Foley, Ph.D.   SERIES EDITOR

Also in the series

Substance Abuse and Family Therapy   Edward Kaufman, M.D.
Structural Family Therapy   Carter C. Umbarger, Ph.D.

Treating the Borderline Family
A Systemic Approach

Craig Everett, Ph.D.
Private Practice and Director,
Arizona Institute of Family Therapy,
Tucson, Arizona

Sandra Halperin, Ph.D.
Private Practice,
Auburn, Alabama

Sandra Volgy, Ph.D.
Private Practice,
Tucson, Arizona

Anne Wissler, M.S.W.
Private Practice,
Decatur, Georgia

Forewords by Allan Beigel, M.D.
Vincent D. Foley, Ph.D.

THE PSYCHOLOGICAL CORPORATION
HARCOURT BRACE JOVANOVICH, INC.

To our former students
and colleagues.

Library of Congress Catalog Number 88-63150
International Standard Book Number 0-15-896062-9
Printed in the United States of America
1 2 3 4 5 6 7 8 9 10 11 12 A B C D E

CONTENTS

FOREWORD

One of the more fascinating areas of study in mental health is the relationship between shifts in society and categories of pathology. It has been suggested that the classic neurotic patient observed by Sigmund Freud was due in large measure to the restrictive climate of the closing decades of the 19th century. Today such patients are rarely seen in clinical practice.

In the closing decades of the 20th century a more common patient is the so called "borderline." At one time such a patient was thought to be beyond help, but an increase in the study of the borderline disorder has brought new hope to such patients. Psychiatric literature reflects an increase in research into the borderline disorder and many psychiatrists have made significant contributions in this area. Gerald Adler, Donald Rinsley and Otto Kernberg have developed their reputations by working with borderline patients, offering new ways of conceptualizing the pathology and suggesting more effective treatment methodologies. Their focus, however, has been largely on the identified patient with the family being observed only in the background.

Although the influence of family therapy has grown substantially in recent decades, it has contributed little to the treatment of borderline patients. Family therapy is regarded as one of a variety of approaches offering no special insight into treatment of the borderline individual.* This is very unfortunate in light of the fact that all agree on the existence of an intense, symbiotic relationship between the borderline individual and family. Although the family is important in the development of any pathology, its role in the development of the borderline disorder is even more critical. Nevertheless one seeks in vain in the family therapy literature for an in-depth study of the borderline disorder. This text is an attempt to fill that void. It is written in the hope that it will reach a wide audience, embracing both those whose approach is the individual and those whose approach is the family. The purpose is to break down the false dichotomy that regards treatment as an either/or situation in which therapists choose sides between the identified patient and the family.

* Hartoclis, P. (Ed.). (1977). *Borderline Personality Disorders.* New York: International University Press.

Many years ago, when I was a struggling young family therapist, I had the good fortune of having the late Nathan Akerman as my supervisor. He pointed out that the role of the therapist was to bring information across boundries from one person to another. It was his feeling that members of a family often were unable to do this for each other. The exchange of such information, he felt, could lead to change by allowing people to see things in a new light. While reading this book I was reminded of Dr. Ackerman's words and I can think of no finer compliment than to say that this work succeeds in bringing information across the boundary between psychiatry and family therapy. Dr. Everett and his associates have built a bridge that allows each viewpoint access to the other.

As therapists, we have been overwhelmed by the quantity of material being published. Most of what is written is repetitious and state the obvious. It does not stretch our minds, nor challenge our assumptions. This book is different. It leads us to see a new way of thinking and working. It is a subtle blend of theory and practice based on over 200 cases with borderline patients. We have, in this book, the distillation of wisdom gleaned over a 10 year period. It is an excellent addition to the Foley Series and should reach a wide spectrum of therapists.

Vincent Foley
Jamaica Estates, New York
October 1988

FOREWORD ——————————————————————

Treating the Borderline Family: A Systemic Approach breaks important new ground in the search for effective treatments for borderline patients. As the diagnostic criteria for this group of mentally disordered persons have been sharpened during the past decade through DSM III and DSM III-R, we have begun to recognize that achieving a greater understanding of phenomenonology does not automatically guarantee e- qual progress in acquiring insight into what needs to occur in order to bring about changes in behavior. Craig Everett, Sandra Halperin, Sandra Volgy, and Ann Wissler present strong evidence that one approach to effective therapeutic intervention lies in a recognition that "the family system forms both a multigenerational etiology and a milieu for maintaining identifiable clinical borderline behaviors."

The work presented in this volume challenges all ther- apists to actively involve the family in the treatment of the borderline patient, since conventional approaches are often "limited to identifying the borderline individual's symptomatology and dynamics within the family setting and to suggesting the occasional use of family interviews as ad- junctive to ongoing individual psychotherapy." With the as- sistance of the clinical material presented here and the guide- lines for therapeutic intervention provided by Everett, Halperin,

Volgy, and Wissler, therapists will have the opportunity to do more than "manage the potential interference by family members during the course of individual treatment."

The value of this work is that it provides scientific data, through the medium of well-documented case studies, to support the authors' contention that "borderline dynamics [go] beyond the behaviors of any one individual and define the borderline condition as a dysfunction of the entire system." Furthermore, in recognizing that the family system of any single generation is influenced by the family systems of previous generations, the authors have emphasized that the individual psychodynamic orientation of classical Freudian theory has a parallel application in understanding how the "sins" of one generation may be visited upon another.

The clinical material and the discussion of therapeutic interventions are presented in a straightforward manner that allows all therapists, regardless of disciplinary origins and training philosophy, to benefit. At the same time, the authors make it clear that considerable training and practical experience under qualified supervision are necessary before any therapist embarks on utilizing family therapy as the treatment of choice for the borderline patient and borderline family. Thus, the reader must recognize that familiarity with the content of this volume does not provide a guarantee of therapeutic success with a very difficult group of patients, but rather serves as an introduction to a new approach to therapy which can be beneficial in practice after training and supervision.

The pearls of dynamic understanding and therapeutic insight which the authors provide are evident from the earliest pages of this book to its closing chapter. From an initial analysis of the difficulties which individual psychotherapy creates in dealing with borderline patients, including transference problems and the instability of the therapeutic alliance, to the final insightful recognition of the special therapeutic resource that a hospital can offer as a "system in and of itself," the reader moves rapidly through a panapoly of subjects which first defines what the borderline family is, then shares a clinical model before discussing treatment strategies. In each chapter, there is a rich supply of clinical material which illustrates the theoretical emphases and helps the reader to relate the material being covered to his or her own practice. The authors have been careful to select case material which is "typical" of the situations most therapists encounter in their practices.

All therapists should be indebted to Everett, Halperin, Volgy, and Wissler for their thoughtful analysis of one of the most difficult therapeutic problems faced today—the borderline patient—and for their recognition that a therapeutic approach through the family may offer new avenues, previously unexplored by most therapists, for treatment success.

Allan Beigel

Allan Beigel is a nationally recognized psychiatrist who is both Professor of Psychiatry and Professor of Psychology at the University of Arizona in Tucson. He is a member of the Institute of Medicine of the National Academy of Sciences and also serves as an officer of the American Psychiatric Association, the American College of Psychiatrists and the Group for the Advancement of Psychiatry.

The borderline condition has been widely discussed in the psychiatry literature over the past decade. During this period, clinical data have become available to refine the definition and identification of this dysfunction into a relatively clear diagnostic category. Consistent with traditional diagnostic criteria in psychiatry, the borderline condition has been defined according to aspects of individual development and behavior with the etiology focused on deficits in early object relations. Much of the available literature in psychiatry addresses both the difficulties of achieving psychotherapeutic change with borderline clients and the challenge of managing ongoing clinical issues of attachment and projection, as well as transferential and countertransferential problems experienced by the therapist in individual psychotherapy.

It has been perplexing for the authors to observe that the evolving and now widely recognized field of family therapy has not yet addressed the clinical phenomena of the borderline condition. Discussion has been limited to identifying the borderline individual's symptomatology and dynamics within the family setting and suggesting the occasional use of family "interviews" as an adjunct to ongoing individual psychotherapy. The rationale for such adjunctive family sessions is to "manage" the potential interference by family members during the course of individual treatment of the identified borderline patient.

It is apparent that the theoretical and clinical resources of family therapy have had very little influence on the borderline literature in psychiatry. Similarly, psychiatry's extensive focus on the borderline condition has not as yet challenged or interfaced with family therapy. Thus, this work is intended to begin a dialogue and perhaps to evolve a linkage between psychiatry and family systems therapy through the integration of clinical data and theoretical concepts.

This work has evolved over a period of nearly 10 years from the experiences of the four authors as family therapists practicing in a variety of clinical settings. Thus we will present the borderline condition from a different orientation than that in the traditional psychiatric literature. We will explain our belief that the family system forms both a multi-generational etiology and a milieu for maintaining identifiable clinical borderline behaviors. We will trace developmental and systemic patterns from which borderline dynamics evolve that go beyond the behaviors of any one individual and define the borderline condition as a dysfunction of the entire family system. We will review the aforementioned problems of individual psychotherapy with borderline clients and reconceptualize these issues as a basis for recommending systemic family therapy as the treatment of choice.

The goal of this work, based on the 10 years of accumulated clinical data, has been to build upon the recognized psychiatric definition of the borderline condition, and through a radical reconceptualization of the disorder from a transgenerational family systems perspective, to evolve a more clinically useful theory upon which to generate data and develop therapeutic strategies. The development of this work has involved a careful analysis of existing psychiatric theory and data and their integration with systemic theory and clinical family data. Our purpose is to propose a model of borderline etiology and to define dynamics which suggest a discernible clinical typology that we have termed the *borderline family*.

While it is hoped that this work will challenge both clinicians and researchers across the mental health disciplines, it is directed toward the practitioner. Fellow clini-

cians who have struggled with both the therapeutic and subjective difficulties of treating the borderline condition will
gain some new "handles" and working hypotheses. We have
written this for practicing family therapists and nonfamily
therapists alike. However, for the latter readers, it should
serve as an introduction to the resources and clinical bene-
fits of utilizing family therapy strategies with special psychiatric disorders.

The approach will be straightforward and focused on
specific clinical issues of assessment and treatment with extensive case analyses in each of the three clinical chapters.
The goal is to provide the clinician with an understanding of
borderline family dynamics that will aid in clinical assessment and treatment and in ongoing family therapy.

Chapter 1 identifies the role of the therapist and inherent problems in working with borderline individuals and
families. It also provides a brief review of the traditional
psychiatric literature defining the borderline condition.
Chapter 2 organizes clinical data from our study and the
literature into a broad systemic model, which suggests a
multi-generational etiology through the transmission of interactional characteristics. Chapter 3 identifies the clinical
features in the assessment of the borderline family, while
Chapter 4 presents the clinical strategies for the planning of
family therapy. Since many borderline individuals may require hospitalization at some stage, Chapter 5 discusses the
special problems of community family therapists working
with inpatient treatment teams. Chapter 6 provides a review
and summary of the work with suggestions for further
research and directions.

An appendix is included to enhance the definition and
understanding of concepts and terms used in this work. We
have included descriptive clinical concepts that evolved from
our study as well as terms from systemic family theory that
may not be familiar to all readers.

This work is based on a project that began in 1978 when
two of the authors (Everett and Halperin), both on the faculty
of an accredited graduate program in family therapy, recognized similarities in the dynamics of borderline cases in their
own practices and among the cases presented for supervision by their clinical students. These two authors began following the identified borderline clients in the context of their

family systems and embarked on co-therapy in several of these cases. The observations from these early clinical experiences were intriguing enough to warrant the organization of a more structured and ongoing clinical investigation. Hugo Zee, M.D., a Menninger-trained psychoanalyst, then on the staff of the well-known Bradley Psychiatric Center in Columbus, Georgia, and now a member of the faculty of the Medical School at Emory University, was invited to participate as a consultant in the early stages of the project in order to broaden our diagnostic skills in identifying borderline individuals.

As we accumulated data from these borderline cases across a broad spectrum of clinical settings (these included both the authors' practices and cases in treatment with graduate students and other therapists in supervision), we began to recognize strikingly similar dynamics in the identified borderline clients' individual development and marital patterns and even in parent–child interactions. At this stage of the project, two colleagues joined us. They added to our clinical data and assisted in the elaboration of our findings. One colleague (Volgy), a family therapist with a background as a clinical child psychologist, examined the parent–child developmental and interactional patterns in both the family of origin and nuclear borderline systems. The other colleague (Wissler), a family therapist with a background as a clinical social worker, evaluated data and conceptualized treatment from the perspective of a therapist practicing in an inpatient psychiatric setting.

The findings of this project, upon which the theoretical model of this work is based, have evolved from over 200 borderline cases across a span of nearly 10 years. We certainly recognize the limitations of utilizing primarily descriptive clinical data in the development of conceptual and theoretical models. However, we have made every effort to integrate our findings with published psychiatric data and recognized clinical patterns. In addition, we have attempted to carefully structure and scrutinize our findings. However, no empirical measures were utilized beyond routine Minnesota Multiphasic Personality Inventories and psychiatric evaluations. The majority of psychometric measures available in the mental health fields are neither designed for nor sensitive to the reciprocal interplay among members of a family system. The few instruments that are emerging which purport to measure dynamics of family functioning have not been tested typically on highly dysfunctioning psychiatric populations. It is our hope that, as the field of family therapy evolves further, it will be possible to employ more structured instrumentation in order to provide a more objective empirical database to further confirm these observations.

Chapter 1

Treating the Borderline Family: An Introduction

When mental health professionals discuss their most frustrating and problematic clients, they are usually talking about borderline individuals. Many therapists, particularly those in private practice, have reported to us that they simply will no longer work with borderline clients because of typical case management difficulties and the stress that such cases place on them. This chapter will discuss these subjective and clinical problems and provide a brief review of the literature on the borderline condition.

THE ROLE AND PREPARATION OF THE FAMILY THERAPIST

This work will develop a rationale for and define applied procedures of family therapy as the treatment of choice for borderline families. However, even the well-trained and seasoned family therapist will struggle with the intensity of primitive emotions and the potential for subjective reactivity that can occur in treating these families. Throughout this work, we will call attention to the role of the family therapist

1

and the potential traps and vulnerabilities inherent in working with borderline families. We believe strongly that any therapist treating borderline families must monitor carefully his or her own susceptibility to subjective reactions of anger or withdrawal. As will be described later, we have seen many cases over the years in which the naiveté or inadequacies of therapists have contributed to destructive and damaging consequences for family members and, occasionally, for the therapists themselves. We cannot overstate the need for personal awareness and responsibility in treating borderline families. Few cases will present the intensity, power, manipulativeness, and drama found in borderline families. Thus it is important to identify patterns of patient/family symptomatology and therapists' response at the outset so that the reader can use them as a reference point throughout the text (Table 1–1).

Table 1–1
DIFFICULTIES ENCOUNTERED IN TREATING
BORDERLINE INDIVIDUALS AND FAMILIES

Case management issues
anger and rage
impulsivity
acting out
manipulation
explosiveness and violence
splitting
projective identification
suicidal threats and actions
idealization
alcohol and drug use

Therapist's response issues (countertransference)
loss of therapeutic control
subjective reactivity
anger
retaliation
seduction
rejection
devaluation
avoidance
displacement onto family members and/or
     colleagues

We would like to recommend strongly that beginning therapists, individual or family oriented, enter into therapy with borderline families only under circumstances in which a clinically structured therapeutic setting is available along with ongoing, weekly, personal supervision from seasoned therapists. As was indicated, we have seen too many cases in which inexperienced therapists failed to recognize the enormous reactive potential of a borderline family and pushed the system to the point where dramatic episodes of impulsive acting-out, suicidal or homicidal behavior, and marital dissolution occurred. One such therapist was accosted at his front door by a borderline mother fearful that the therapist was acting to remove her favored child from the family—she plunged a letter opener between his ribs. We have also seen many experienced therapists who have committed ethical violations when therapeutic boundaries eroded and emotional and physical relationships evolved with their borderline clients.

It should not be surprising that therapists who treat borderline families become susceptible and responsive to the very intensity that defines the borderline system. This is why we have cited a great deal of psychiatric literature dealing with countertransference. However, from the point of view of the family therapist, the object of therapeutic treatment is not simply the presenting individual but rather the family system and its reciprocal interactive patterns involving all other members. Thus the phenomenon of countertransference recognized in the process of individual psychotherapy must be broadened to reflect the family therapist's engagement with both an array of individuals and the family system itself. Slipp (1980) has observed that "In working with [borderline] couples and families, there is a greater possibility of being sucked into a countertransference reaction than in individual therapy; the complexity of the field and presence of a triad tend to foster splitting" (p. 255).

Ackerman (1958) defined the traditional concept of countertransference for the family therapist as a subjective reactivity by the therapist toward the family in treatment that may occur on at least two levels. In one situation the therapist may respond to specific traits of the clinical family which trigger similarities with or a repetition of dynamics from within his or her own family of origin. These features may either seduce the therapist into the system, causing loss of objectivity and control, or cause the therapist to withdraw and pull away, with loss of engagement. On the other hand, the therapist may simply be reacting to the specific dynamics experienced in the treatment process with the family (*objective countertransference*).

In treating the borderline family either of these patterns of subjective reactivity may occur. For the less experienced therapist, it is not uncommon for aspects of both levels of reactivity to occur simultaneously in the same case. The unique tandem defenses of splitting and projective identification (these will be discussed further at the end of this chapter) displayed by borderline individuals and families tend to challenge the therapist's own management skills. Splitting represents a preambivalent process whereby the "good" and "bad" aspects of a personal object are not integrated, and the object is perceived alternately as "all good" and "all bad." Projective identification involves the projection of unacceptable aspects of oneself onto another close object resulting in identification with or reaction to these attributes perceived in that person. The split aspects of an object and these projected unacceptable components of an individual may be projected onto other family members as well as onto a therapist. These defensive features characterize the central interactive patterns of borderline families and present the major difficulties in conducting therapy.

The most common reactive responses experienced by therapists treating borderline families are those of anger and aggression. Here the family's projection of hostile and aggressive feelings onto the therapist is gradually "accepted" by the therapist, who then begins to feel unusually hostile toward the family even though outwardly the system itself does not appear to deserve such a response. This often occurs when the therapist is also being devalued by family members, which often increases the therapist's vulnerability to "accepting" these projections.

The drama and subtlety of these countertransference-like reactions may be even more intense in family therapy with borderline systems than in the traditional individual treatment model. When the individual therapist enters into a therapeutic relationship with a single client a type of dyadic-interactive system is created. Dynamics related to the history of the family and the actual interactive patterns with other members are secondary and adjunctive to the immediacy of this dyadic therapeutic relationship. When a family therapist engages a borderline family system, he or she in effect interfaces with and attempts to join the ongoing history of the family and its multiple interactive patterns. The therapist not only must experience clinically the moods and dynamics of the family members but must also achieve some therapeutic management of their chaos.

It is this process of joining the borderline family's system that enhances the intensity and thus potential vulnerability of the therapist for personal reactivity. In individual psychotherapy the odds of maintaining therapeutic control favor the therapist since the process is based on a one-on-one relationship. For the family therapist the control issue involves the clinical management of multiple members of the family system.

For example, in one case a therapist found herself becoming confrontative and harsh with a borderline mother, telling her that she did not believe that she could ever become a nurturing mother to her children. When the therapist reviewed this with her supervisor she acknowledged feeling guilty as soon as she spoke these words and could not understand why she would make such an unempathic and even destructive comment to the mother. While this interaction was completely out of character for this therapist, she recognized her anger at the mother and the family for devaluing her role and efforts with them. She reported that she had never felt so "out of control" therapeutically before.

In another similar situation where co-therapists were working with a borderline family, one of the therapists became very angry with the mother who was praising a day care program's success with her child and accusing the therapist of wasting her time and money. During this session, due to the projective dynamic, the mother appeared rather calm and controlled while the therapist became, again uncommonly, passive-aggressive. The co-therapist intervened to end the session before it became more destructive. Following the session, before they met with their supervisor, both therapists reported being confused and angry, initially with one another and then with the family.

In such situations it is not uncommon for the therapist to become the "bad" object for a family in a splitting and projective maneuver. When this occurs there is nothing a therapist can do or say that can be accepted as constructive or good by the family. The therapist is devalued and begins to feel worthless and helpless in working with the family.

Another such case involved a hospitalized borderline mother, her husband, and three children. Following the hospitalization, the mother engaged in splitting and projection as follows: the inpatient therapist became the "good" therapist/object; and the family therapist, the "bad" therapist/object. She berated the family therapist for being inexperienced (she was younger than the inpatient therapist) and accused her of being unable to do anything productive or helpful for her family. During the therapy sessions in the hospital the rest of the family sat passively watching the mother's attack on the therapist. After each session the therapist emerged feeling increasingly helpless and impotent. Soon she began to doubt that she should even be working with families and became clinically depressed.

These cases illustrate both the difficult struggle for therapeutic control and continuity and the boundary problems for the therapist resulting in over-reactivity or subjective devaluation. In contrasting situations the therapist may become the "good" object with the resultant experience of idealization by the family. The therapist may feel that the case is "under control" and indeed that he or she can do no wrong therapeutically. In these situations the therapist is gradually seduced into controlling the system on the family's terms, compromising both objectivity and control. Because all of us like to hear praise and want to be liked, we all are susceptible to this trap.

Unfortunately, while we may feel closer and more "joined" with the family and perhaps even "successful" in getting beyond what other therapists have been able to do, we fail to recognize the subtle escalation of intensity and stress that signal an impending crisis. When such a crisis occurs, the role of the therapist may typically shift to that of the "bad" object. In fact we have observed that in the majority of cases, during the early phases of therapy, the projection of "good" and "bad" onto the therapist may actually alternate from week to week. This of course leads to considerable confusion as well as a sense of impotence on the part of the therapist and renders the achievement of therapeutic continuity problematic.

From these examples it should be clear that the treatment of a borderline family will challenge the therapist's personal and clinical preparation. Few other types of cases along the entire spectrum of clinical practice will present the perplexing array of intensity, power, manipulation, chaos, splitting, and projection. Thus the therapist must be prepared, both personally and through consultation and supervision, to contain the emotional intensity and subjective reactivity inherent in this clinical work. *A hallmark of the borderline family is that it has failed as a crucible in which aggression is tempered.* Aggression in these family systems is denied and passed across generations via splitting and projection. In the therapy experience, it is disowned and passed on to the therapist. Early in the therapy process with borderline families the therapist must be able to tolerate a certain amount of "dumping" of aggression in order to successfully evolve a therapeutic structure and attain a therapeutic alliance. The therapist must draw on considerable personal and clinical resources in order to model a reflective rather than reactive role with the family which can allow conflict and tolerate certain levels of deviance, manipulativeness, and aggression.

It is through these experiences of containment and understanding by the therapist that the borderline family members will become less fearful and able to begin to "own" their aggression. At a later stage, the therapist will be able to reflect more subjective reactions back to the family; e.g., "I wonder if you are trying to make me feel impotent since you feel so angry that there are no easy solutions." However, this more direct reflection would not be tolerated by a borderline system early in therapy.

It must be recognized that the therapist who has difficulty with conflict and aggression by virtue of personality traits or family of origin experiences may not be able to treat borderline families effectively. We have consulted with many therapists in both private practice settings and mental health facilities who report that they have become intimidated by such cases as well as feeling "burned out" and doubting their worth and effectiveness as therapists.

We often recommend, particularly for less seasoned therapists, the use of co-therapy teams of family therapists in working with borderline families. This serves to dilute and better manage some of the intensity and aggression and allows the therapists to support one another in reality testing and encouragement when subjective devaluation becomes too great. It is particularly useful when a co-therapist can help identify quickly a colleague's acceptance of a projection or early subjective reactivity and thus allow him or her to modify this response before the end of a session.

Many therapists work in private practice settings where co-therapy is often not feasible, and they are perhaps even more vulnerable to these stressors than those who have colleagues available in an agency setting. Thus we recommend strongly the development of collegial support systems and ongoing supervision to provide for as much reality testing and emotional support as possible when treating borderline families.

In addition to professional vulnerability, the treatment of borderline families has the potential to make therapists behave in a "crazy" manner too. Reactive periods of anger or depression will have obvious detrimental effects on the therapist's own relationships and family system. It is not at all unusual for the intensity and often primitiveness of borderline behaviors to trigger latent unresolved personal and family of origin issues for many therapists, particularly the less experienced. Some therapists may re-enter therapy themselves in order to resolve these formerly latent issues or to enhance their own personal resources and ego strength, which may be challenged by the intensity of this work.

Few cases across the broad spectrum of clinical practice will challenge the therapist's skills and personal resources as intensely as the borderline family. Thus we have tried to identify both the theoretical and the technical issues involved in assessment and treatment and the potential problems that may evoke subjective vulnerabilities for the therapist.

PROBLEMS IN INDIVIDUALLY ORIENTED PSYCHOTHERAPY

As we have indicated, the majority of literature on the treatment of the borderline condition has failed to identify the intrinsic involvement of family dynamics and has not utilized the clinical resources of family therapy. In such literature, family therapy is typically defined only as an "adjunct" to traditional individual psychotherapy or as a "mechanism" for managing the family's potential interference with the individual treatment of the identified borderline member. Such an orientation reflects a clinical stance that focuses fundamentally on the individual client. This individual orientation may recognize "external influences" from family members or other sources, but does not take the next step necessary in reconceptualizing the individual within the bonding and reciprocity of the family system itself. This means that the family therapist begins an assessment by looking for the broader interactive patterns of the family system, even as they may occur across several generations, rather than focusing initially or solely on the presenting individual dynamics of a single client. This perspective, which we will describe later in this chapter, identifies the uniqueness of a family systems orientation.

Since it is our position that family therapy can become the treatment of choice for borderline families, it is important for the reader to recognize that such a treatment stance involves an orientation regarding symptoms and behaviors that is dramatically different from that learned in training and socialization for individual psychotherapy. Family therapy involves a shift in orientation (epistemology) such that the therapist engages the broader circular and reciprocal interactive patterns of the system rather than focusing solely on individual behaviors or symptoms. As we will discuss, family therapy involves more than adding a new treatment intervention or technique to one's clinical repertoire; it involves approaching one's practice from a new stance.

However, since the majority of clinical reports on the treatment of the borderline condition identify individual psychotherapy as the treatment of choice (e.g., Waldinger & Gunderson, 1987), it is important to recognize the issues and difficulties that have been encountered by individually oriented psychotherapists. Early psychoanalytic authors such as Oberndorf (1948) and Eisenstein (1951) suggested that many of the clinical failures of psychoanalysis involve the treatment of borderline individuals. These failures occur despite the fact that psychoanalytic theory has contributed major clinical data and conceptual resources to the understanding and definition of the borderline syndrome.

The basic difficulties identified by the literature in conducting individual psychotherapy with a borderline patient fall into two categories: (1) transference problems related to the client's poor ego development, and (2) splitting and projective identification, which inhibit the development of a therapeutic alliance. Eisenstein (1951) reported that, unlike a "neurotic" client, the borderline individual does not possess sufficient ego development or "emotional contact" to enter a therapeutic process directed toward internal change. Adler (1980) described the typical borderline client in psychotherapy as struggling between wishes for nurturance from the therapist/object and the fear of loss of self in a merger with the therapist due to a breakdown of ego boundaries. He reports: "For this kind of patient, the dyadic relationship offered by the therapist elicits increased longings and leads to an emergence of anger, rage, and envy, as disappointments from the past readily become alive in the often rapidly evolving transference" (p. 172).

This reactivity of the borderline client in the transference process has been described by Eisenstein (1951) as unpredictable and reaching "passionately childish levels of expression" (p. 314). Searles (1986) describes a nonhuman quality in borderline clients' responses to the therapist; they often react to therapists as if they were "nonexistent, or a corpse, or a pervasive and sinister supernatural force" (p. 29). Similarly, Nadelson (1976) has identified aggression as the "pivotal issue to be confronted by the therapist in treatment of borderline conditions" (p. 126). He suggests that this aggression will trigger in the therapist an impulse to counterattack.

The borderline client's use of splitting and projective identification becomes equally problematic for the individually oriented therapist. In the context of the therapy process, the borderline individual is unable to integrate both positive and negative aspects of the same internalized object. The client then becomes inordinately sensitive to minor frustrations with the therapist. As a result, the client relinquishes positive perceptions and begins to experience the therapist as attacking and rejecting. According to Shapiro and colleagues (1975), the client must then respond defensively toward the therapist to control this projected rage: "The urgent need to control a therapist distorted by aggressive projections interferes with the patient's ability to use him in the work of examining and integrating behavior" (p. 77). This experience leads to what Chessick (1972) has defined as one of the "thorniest problems in the psychotherapy of the borderline patient"—the determination of limits.

Kernberg (1968, 1975) has observed that the borderline client projects onto the therapist a sense of uselessness, lack of worth, or hostility. It is this projective identification in the therapeutic relationship that creates the ongoing dilemma for the therapist. While projection leads to the rejection of the object, the primitive aspects of projective identification lead to a diffusion of ego boundaries. Thus identification occurs with the therapist on whom the aggressive feelings have been projected, and in the transference relationship the therapist is experienced as hostile and attacking (Nadelson, 1976). Here the client perceives the hostility to be self-protective and enters into a "sadistic" power struggle with the therapist (Malin & Grotstein, 1966).

These dynamics lead to obvious problems in the development of a therapeutic alliance in individual psychotherapy with the borderline client. This struggle to achieve a therapeutic relationship involves the reciprocal roles of "victim" and "victimizer" (Masterson & Rinsley, 1975; Nadelson, 1976). Nadelson suggested that the therapist is subjected to a "continuing siege of projections and projective identifications"(p.115)andcautionsagainst"repetitivesadomasochistic interactions" (p. 115). Shapiro et al. (1975) have identified the therapeutic task as "a constant struggle to keep in the foreground enough of the working alliance to limit this destructive use of splitting and projection of unmodified rage" (pp. 77–78).

The therapeutic alliance may be jeopardized further by the borderline client's experience of therapeutic change as "giving in" to the control or power of the therapist. Rosner (1969) observed that such potential movement triggers the threat of loss of self in the borderline individual, who equates change with potential abandonment.

All of these problematic features of engaging a borderline client in individual psychotherapy convey clearly not only the intensity of this therapeutic process but also the potential for the therapist's own subjective reactivity toward the client to become operationalized in the therapy setting. One therapist has suggested that therapy should consist only of regular but limited and infrequent sessions with the borderline client simply to assist in managing the therapist's own "countertransference" (Zetzel, 1971).

The therapist's vulnerability to countertransference anger, based on the emergence of the borderline client's aggression from within the therapist, is identified throughout the literature (Fine, 1985; Kernberg, 1968; Maltsberger & Buie, 1972; Masterson, 1983; Nadelson, 1976; Wolberg, 1982). The occasional barrage of demeaning and angry attacks directed by the borderline client toward the therapist can be overwhelming, particularly to the inexperienced. The intensity of these attacks may trigger a typical countertransference response or the reaction may simply be an angry response to a stress-specific situation. It has been our observation that even well-integrated and seasoned therapists will experience these reactions to such attacks. Nadelson (1976) identifies these latter responses as "normal" or "objective" countertransference, indicating that it is an expectable human response and that all therapists treating borderline clients are susceptible.

In managing the explicit projective defenses, Nadelson (1976) observed that the therapist may be aware only of the client's projection *onto* him or her and may remain unaware of the client's projected feeling within him or her. He has termed this response by the therapist to projective identification "projective counteridentification."

While some therapists may react to the borderline client with anger, as we have noted, others may disengage and withdraw from the therapeutic relationship. Masterson (1983) identified the therapist's characteristic responses as helplessness, overdirectiveness, and guilt. Nadelson (1976) suggests that the therapist must react to his or her discomfort with self-examination rather than distancing: "Often it is necessary to realize, repeatedly, that he [the therapist] is subject to emotional forces which at times are too difficult for immediate mastery, that he wishes to help as best he can, that the patient is defending against a sense of vulnerability (rather than being simply an aggressive, hostile person) and that he also defends for the same reason" (p. 121).

For these reasons, it is difficult to establish a therapeutic alliance and conduct ongoing individual psycho-therapy with a borderline client. Additional problems may arise for the therapist who struggles to treat the borderline individual in isolation from the family system. For example, the therapist who works with a borderline client in individual therapy often fails to recognize the intrusive power of the client's family system. By focusing solely on the intensity and drama of the borderline individual's symptomatology rather than the broader interactive and reciprocal family dynamics, the therapist fails to recognize that it is the family system itself which creates the dysfunctional milieu into which the symptomatic individual must fit (Mandelbaum, 1980). Slipp (1980) has observed that the borderline in-dividual's use of projective identification in the therapy process evolves from the identification with the family sys-tem's own defenses and not solely from within the psyche.

Thus, when an adult family member displaying border-line symptomatology enters individual psychotherapy, reciprocal family loyalties and the structural balance of the family system will dictate the range of potential therapeutic improvement or change. As an example, a 40-year-old female diagnosed as borderline had been in individual therapy with four different male therapists over a 10-year period. In each therapeutic relationship she appeared to sabotage the therapy by either emotionally or sexually seducing the therapist. No sequence of therapy had lasted longer than 1 year. At the age of 40, during a depressive and suicidal period, she entered therapy again at the urging of her hus-band (who happened to be one of her former therapists). She entered therapy on this occasion with a female therapist and made good progress over an 18-month period. Gradually she began to "own" and manage some of her aggression more directly within the family.

At this point her growth began to unbalance the stereotypical dynamics within the system, and family mem-bers began to feel threatened and resisted further change. Soon family members even made threats toward the therapist. It became apparent that the splitting and projec-tive components of the family system remained powerful despite the growth of the borderline individual. It was clear that even though the individual client had begun to change, some patterns within the family system itself would have to change if further improvement were to take place.

The therapist decided to terminate individual treatment with the borderline client and refer the case to a family therapist. The family, particularly the husband, became outraged, stating that the wife was the "psychotic" one. The husband refused to enter family therapy and began to make covert threats to manipulate the individual therapist to take the wife back into treatment. When the therapist refused, the husband searched frantically for another therapist who would see the wife individually. This case highlights the power of the family system, the collective nature of the symptomatic components, and the need for the therapist not just to be aware of but also to gain therapeutic access to the entire system.

Similar difficulties may occur in a different clinical scenario in which the individually oriented therapist accepts an acting-out child into therapy without conducting a thorough assessment of the child's family system. We believe that many clinical failures in treating angry, disruptive, and threatening children/adolescents may arise from the therapist's own failure to recognize that the child's behavior is simply one component of what we will define as a powerful borderline family system. Here the therapeutic focus on the child's disruptive behaviors in isolation from the family system simply serves to reinforce and maintain the splitting and projective functions and resultant roles within the system itself.

The potential trap for the therapist in this situation is that the parents who bring the child for therapy may appear rather functional. Predictably, efforts to treat the acting-out child individually will progress only until therapeutic progress in the child threatens the tenuous homeostatic balance of the family system. In fact, individual therapeutic alliances with children of borderline families remain tenuous at best because the intensity of the family's functioning dramatically binds the child's loyalties to the system. Thus if the child makes changes beyond a limited range of accommodation acceptable to the system, the family will intensify its loyalty demands. A subtle threat of abandonment ensues and the child is effectively pulled out of therapy and back within the homeostatic control of the system. We have observed cases in which an acting-out child, or what we will later describe as the persecuting child, has repeatedly been pulled in and out of therapy with different therapists and agencies. Unfortunately, most of these therapists never recognized or looked for the sabotaging process within the family system.

Thus it is not uncommon that influences from within the family system may confuse and sabotage the therapeutic process as dramatically as the more recognized individual dynamics of splitting and projective identification. This is why some individually oriented therapists have recommended the use of "adjunctive" family sessions in an effort to manage what they perceive as "disruptive" (i.e., sabotaging) influences by the family. Such a recommendation is certainly a reasonable response to the intense frustration often experienced by individually oriented therapists who are involved in the treatment of borderline clients. However, it suggests a continuing naiveté regarding family systems therapy because it ignores the reciprocal and recursive dynamics of the family system which define and reinforce the very symptomatology and structural milieu of the borderline individual. The power of the family system in maintaining the borderline dynamics of the individual can ultimately diminish the potential beneficial outcomes of individually oriented therapy and render the therapist clinically impotent and frustrated.

DEFINING THE BORDERLINE CONDITION

The diagnostic category of the borderline condition has evolved from traditional psychiatric studies and treatment experiences which have focused primarily on individual behavior and symptomatology. While the intent of this chapter is to develop a reconceptualization of the borderline phenomenon within the family system, this section will offer a brief overview of the traditional psychiatric literature regarding assessment, differential diagnosis, etiological theory, and borderline defenses.

Assessment Features

The psychiatric literature continues to evidence considerable debate regarding the classification of the borderline diagnosis, with the disorder variously defined as a clinical syndrome, a characterological pattern, a form of personality organization, and more recently, a "condition." Gunderson and Singer (1975) traced the historical development of the borderline concept from an early paper in 1938 to a later paper in 1953. They have concluded that the borderline diagnosis evolved from three early diagnostic classifications: "latent schizophrenia" (Bleuler, 1911), "ambulatory schizophrenia" (Zilborg, 1941), and "as if personality" (Deutsch, 1942). These classifications evolved into "pseudoneurotic schizophrenia," which was the most popular term until "borderline" came into general use.

Clinical efforts to identify specific assessment features have varied widely. An analysis of only four such published efforts identified 104 different assessment criteria (Perry & Klerman, 1978). Even in clinical practice the use of such criteria may be highly variable. A study of 160 psychiatrists reported that such characteristics were more commonly diagnosed "borderline psychotics" when the patient was 12 years of age or less and "borderline personalities" in patients between the ages of 12 and 18 years (Bradley, 1981).

One of the more widely accepted and cited classifications of borderline assessment features was developed by Gunderson and Singer (1975). They identified the following six borderline diagnostic characteristics:

1. Minipsychotic episodes or brief lapses of reality testing.
2. The presence of intense affect, such as anger, hostility, or emptiness.
3. A certain social adaptiveness.
4. A history of impulsive behavior.
5. Loose thinking in unstructured situations.
6. Relationships that vacillate between transient superficiality and intense dependency.

This classification was followed by Gunderson's Diagnostic Interview for Borderline Patients (DIB), which identified numerous assessment criteria organized under five categories: social adaptations, impulse/action patterns, affects, psychosis, and interpersonal relations (Gunderson et al., 1981, Armelius et al., 1985).

The decision to include the borderline designation in the third edition of the *Diagnostic and Statistical Manual of Mental Disorders* (DSM-III) (American Psychiatric Association [APA], 1980) served both to legitimize this condition as an acceptable psychiatric diagnosis and to bring some definition to the formerly broad range of assessment criteria. The recently revised DSM-III-R (APA, 1987) has identified eight assessment criteria, of which any five are considered to be necessary for the diagnosis:

1. A pattern of unstable and intense interpersonal relationships characterized by alternating between extremes of overidealization and devaluation.
2. Impulsivity in at least two areas that are potentially self-damaging, e.g., spending, sex, substance use, shoplifting, reckless driving, binge eating.
3. Affective instability: marked shifts from baseline mood to depression, irritability, or anxiety, usually lasting a few hours and only rarely more than a few days.
4. Inappropriate, intense anger or lack of control of anger, e.g., frequent displays of temper, constant anger, recurrent physical fights.
5. Recurrent suicidal threats, gestures, or behavior, or self-mutilating behavior.
6. Marked and persistent identity disturbances manifested by uncertainty about at least two of the folllowing: self-image, sexual orientation, long-term goals or career choice, type of friends desired, preferred values.
7. Chronic feelings of emptiness or boredom.
8. Frantic efforts to avoid real or imagined abandonment.

Despite the noted classification role of the DSM in the field, there has been considerable debate and disagreement over these criteria. For example, Gunderson and colleagues (1980) were critical of these criteria because they omitted the recognized feature of "brief lapses of reality testing." This was supported by Bradley (1981), who believed that this was an essential criterion "in distinguishing the borderline from other types of related characterological pathology" (p. 125).

Ongoing clinical study will be necessary to provide further refinement of the diagnosis of the borderline condition.

Differential Diagnosis

Several clinical reports have attempted to identify differential diagnostic components for the borderline condition in comparison with other psychiatric diagnoses. (The reader is referred to other major works on the borderline condition for a more comprehensive analysis, e.g., Grinker & Werble, 1977; Kernberg, 1975; Masterson, 1976, 1983; Searles, 1986; Wolberg, 1982.) Gunderson and Kolb (1978) attempted to identify discriminate characteristics of borderline subjects upon inpatient admission in contrast to groups of diagnosed schizophrenics, neurotic depressives, and a broad mixed grouping. They reported that the schizophrenic group was characterized consistently by flat affect, derealization, and social isolation in contrast to the borderline group, which displayed a consistent pattern of social aggressiveness, devaluation, and manipulation in interpersonal relationships, and a high frequency of drug abuse and psychotic experiences associated with the drug use. In comparison with the depressive group, the borderline individuals displayed a consistently higher frequency of dysphoria and anhedonia, brief paranoid experiences, sexual deviancy directed toward promiscuity, lower school and work achievement, intolerance to being alone, unstable interpersonal relationships, and again, drug abuse associated with psychotic experiences.

Gunderson and Kolb (1978) classified fourteen characteristic borderline variables into seven discriminate clinical criteria:

1. Low achievement despite apparent higher abilities.
2. Impulsivity, particularly related to alcohol, drug, and sexual deviancy.
3. Manipulative suicidal gestures to evoke a "saving" response from a significant other.
4. Heightened affectivity, particularly anger.
5. Mild psychotic experiences in a drug-free form of paranoid ideations, derealizations, and regression

during treatment, all in the absence of significant historical psychotic symptoms.

6. High socialization with a compulsive feature to avoid
   being alone.
7. Disturbed close relationships found in intense attachments characterized by the manipulative use of
   somatic complaints and provocative behavior to gain
   control/support, masochism, and dependency.

In a more theoretical report, Adler (1980) attempted to
identify a continuum between borderline and narcissistic
characteristics. He reported that borderline subjects could
be located at one end of a continuum characterized by poor
self-cohesiveness, i.e., feeling unreal, emotionally dull, lacking initiative, depleted, and empty; tenuous self-object
transference ability in therapy; and the failure to achieve
mature aloneness, i.e., emptiness, helplessness, and despair
often accompanied by rage and panic. He suggested that in
successful, long-term individual psychotherapy, the borderline client moves along this continuum, taking on more iden-
tifiably narcissistic features.

Empathy in personal development is often identified as a
differential component in distinguishing between borderline
and nonborderline behavior since it requires the successful
completion of both early symbiotic and separation-individuation tasks. When these early developmental tasks are completed, a child is able to recognize and respond to others as
whole objects who are different yet reliable and predictable
(Rinsley, 1978). The non-borderline or even neurotic individual experiences empathy when he or she recognizes the
similarity and congruence of another's feelings with one's
own. The borderline individual, by comparison, responds to
others with a "distant early warning system" necessary to
guard against the unpredictability and danger that is projected onto or perceived in one's environment. Thus the borderline individual becomes a slave to this "pseudo-empathic"
sensitivity toward the affective messages of others (Carter &
Rinsley, 1977).

As the reader reviews these and other clinical reports, it
becomes apparent that the differential discrimination of the
borderline condition has become quite complex. Even within
the recognized diagnostic classification of the borderline

condition a variety of characteristics and typologies emerge which further complicate the assessment process (Meissner, 1983). For example, Singer (1975) reported "constricted" versus "expansive" borderline types, while Robbins (1976) identified a "compliant" versus an "aggressive" typology. Grinker and Werble (1977) simply said that some borderline individuals could be characterized as having "given up" while others were "still searching."

Rinsley (1978) has differentiated four borderline subtypes. The "psychotic-like" individual displays significant reality and self-identity impairment, inappropriate behavior, hostility toward others, and either underlying depression or psychotic episodes. The "as-if" type displays more intact reality, self-identity, and adaptability with patterns of pseudo-compliance, pseudo-intimacy, and pseudo-hostility. The "anaclitic-hysteriform" individual displays more anxiety and depression, helplessness in relationships, and exhibitionistic, provocative, and seductive behaviors. The "pleomorphic" type presents multi-symptomatic neurotic features with somatization and psychosomatic symptoms. All of these differential characteristics are intended to assist the clinician in recognizing and understanding the variable features of the borderline condition.

Etiological Theories of Borderline Development

The etiology of the borderline condition has been viewed broadly as a failure in ego development which occurs during the early childhood stage of separation-individuation. It is widely accepted theoretically that inconsistent object relationship patterns with the mothering figure may interfere with the child's normal movement in the developmental sequence from symbiosis to individuation. Meissner (1978), in a review of the clinical literature, identified six potential etiological factors:

1. Developmental failure
2. Poor object relations
3. Identity diffusion
4. Instinctual defects

5. Defense mechanism impairments
6. Other ego and narcissistic defects

Introduction to Object Relations Theory

Based on these identified factors, it is apparent that the central etiological dynamics of the borderline condition are represented by issues of ego development and object relations. In this work we cannot provide the reader with more than a cursory introduction to object relations theory. However, we would strongly urge clinicians working with borderline families to familiarize themselves with several of the following theorists: Jacobson, 1964; A. Freud, 1965; Guntrip, 1968; Blanck and Blanck, 1974; Kernberg, 1976; and Mahler, 1971.

Briefly, object relations theory identifies the internal images that an individual develops during infancy within the close mothering/parenting relationships (i.e., objects). In normal development, these internal images reflect accurately the reality of the person or close object, and these are available to the infant to be reshaped and redefined by incoming experiences and data. When this normal process is disrupted, these internal images become inflexible, stereotyped, and unamenable to modification by new data.

Historically, object relations theory has emerged from the broader school of ego psychology. This latter movement evolved from traditional psychoanalytic theory in a somewhat dramatic fashion by moving away from Freud's biological determinism and focusing on the centrality of the ego in the context of human relationships. Objects have been defined as "aspects of symbols of people," and Freud viewed the ego as seeking such objects in order to fulfill certain instinctual needs (Mendez & Fine, 1976).

Mendez and Fine (1976), in their historical overview of object relations theory, have observed that it was Melanie Klein (1932) who first broke with Freud's notion that objects never become an internalized part of the psyche. Rather, she suggested, objects are indeed internalized through the process of splitting the maternal object into good and bad objects.

W.R.D. Fairbairn (1952, 1954), certainly a central figure in this movement, posited the development of the ego within the context of human interaction and relationships—a further dramatic step beyond Freud. He suggested that the ego is present at birth, there is no such thing as an "id," the ego is basically object-seeking, and the earliest form of anxiety in the infant is separation anxiety (1963). Internalization of the maternal object occurs as a result of the infant's frustration with the mothering relationship (e.g., availability of the breast), and the exciting and frustrating aspects of this internalized object are split off and repressed, leaving for the ego what is often described as the ego-ideal or ideal object. Thus Fairbairn moved the understanding of ego and personality development beyond Freud's psychosexual theory by defining the central role of the ego's psychosocial milieu and the "necessity of being loved as a person by the significant people in one's life" (see Mendez & Fine, 1976).

Other figures contributing to the understanding of ego development in a psychosocial context include D.W. Winnicott (1965, 1971), Heinz Hartmann (1950), Harry Guntrip (1967, 1971), and John Bowlby (1969, 1973, 1980). Winnicott described the ego as the organizing force of one's personality. He introduced the concept of "good enough mothering" to describe the quality of maternal care necessary for the normal infant's ego to grow and mature. He suggested that this quality could not be taught to someone not possessing it. Hartmann, not as removed as the others from Freud, contributed the understanding of the adaptability of the ego. Guntrip was a synthesizer of the foregoing theories and reinforced the importance of the ego's psychosocial milieu and relationships in the process of growth, the development of selfhood, and interactive competency (see Mendez & Fine, 1976). Bowlby expanded the understanding of this psychosocial and interactive milieu with his contribution of attachment theory. He defined the attachment process and resultant behaviors as central to healthy ego development and believed that the quality of these affectional bonds, initially between infant and mother, form the basis for interactional patterns and attachment throughout adult life.

The primary linkage between object relations theory and the etiology of the borderline condition is found in Margaret Mahler's description of the early developmental attachment process between infant and maternal object (Mahler, 1971; Mahler et al., 1975). Mahler's theory defines a normal developmental progression (see Table 1–2) in infancy from

Table 1–2
PHASES AND SUBPHASES OF MAHLER'S MODEL
OF EARLY INFANT DEVELOPMENT*

Normal autistic phase (first month of life)
Symbiotic phase (2 through 5–6 months)
Separation-individuation phase
    Differentiation and the development of the body image
      (6 through 10 months)
    Practicing (10–12 through 16–18 months)
    Rapprochement (18 through 24 months)
    Consolidation of individuality and the beginnings of emotional
      object constancy (25 through 36 months)

---

*Mahler, 1971, 1975.

stages of symbiosis to separation-individuation to object constancy. During the symbiotic period of 2 to 5 months, the interdependence between mother and infant is complete, with the infant experiencing the mother as one with himself or herself. The infant at this stage experiences a sense of omnipotence with no differentiating boundaries or separateness. Winnicott (1960) described an important aspect of this period as a "holding environment" provided by the mothering object.

The ensuing separation-individuation stage (Mahler et al., 1975) is divided into subphases. The first, differentiation, occurs between 5 and 8 months while the infant is still attached symbiotically to the mother. However, the infant is gradually becoming oriented to external experiences, which can be observed by the smiling response. The practicing subphase is characterized by locomotion when the infant begins gradually to move away from the mother, yet returns quickly for "refueling." At the next subphase of rapprochement, the infant begins to develop clearer boundaries between self and mother, yet with recurring feelings of loneliness and concern over her absence. This is characterized by conflict in the wish for reunion and the fear of engulfment displayed in the infant's shadowing and darting away behavior. As the infant approaches the final stage of object constancy, he or she has learned to tolerate a certain ambivalent image of the mother even in the face of frustration. Here the infant moves from self-centered actions to recognition of other objects, self-confidence, cooperation, and sharing.

Thus, normal developmental progression begins with the differentiation of the self and the object whereby internal boundaries are beginning to be drawn which will separate and define the infant's experiences from the actual experiences of the mothering object. Gradually this leads to object constancy with the infant beginning to accept and "own" the confusing internal experiences of both loving and hating the close object on whom he or she is still dependent. These conflicting and yet simultaneously experienced emotions are in response to the image of the mothering object as both gratifying and frustrating. From this difficult yet normative experiential process evolves the capacity to tolerate separation by maintaining an internal supportive image of the mothering object even during the frustrations of her absences.

Etiological Theory

Mahler's developmental framework provides the foundation for understanding the role of developmental failure in the etiology of the borderline condition. Failure to achieve this level of object constancy means that the infant does not internalize a strong and clear positive image of the mothering object so as to be able to tolerate the experience of the negative interactions without feeling overwhelmed by them. This dynamic identifies theoretically the origin of the borderline condition in the infant who has achieved the prior developmental task of self-object differentiation but failed to master that of object constancy. The result then is an infant, and later adult, who cannot tolerate separation or ambivalence without regression (Shapiro, 1978).

As we have described, in normative development through these early stages the infant evolves what Kernberg (1972) has called an "object relations unit." This unit is derived from these internalizations of the interactions with the mothering object. It is composed of a representation (image) of the self, a representation of the mothering object, and an affective link between these two images. This unit as developed within a borderline individual is theoretically split into two separate parts—a part-self representation and a part-object representation, again with affective linkages.

Rinsley (1978) has characterized these part-units as rejecting and rewarding. The rejecting part-object representation of the mother is experienced as hostile, angry, and withholding. It is associated with the part-self representation of inadequacy, helplessness, guilt, and emptiness. These are linked affectively for the individual by chronic anger, frustration, and abandonment depression. The rewarding part-object representation of goodness, passivity, obedience, and compliance is linked affectively by feeling good and gratification of the wish for reunion. For the borderline individual, these affective components remain separated so that the self and object are perceived persistently as "all good" or "all bad" (Masterson & Rinsley, 1975). Kernberg (1975) has summarized this failure to achieve object constancy as resulting in the continued primitive use of splitting, inadequate integration of self, chronic overdependence on external objects, limited capacity to test reality, intolerance of anxiety and frustration, and inability to attain basic trust in relationships.

The timing of this developmental failure has been debated widely in the literature. Kernberg originally suggested that it occurs during the fourth to twelfth month of infancy (see Masterson & Rinsley, 1975). However, most of the literature now supports Mahler's developmental framework (1971, 1975), which places the crucial period between 16 and 25 months in the rapprochement subphase of the separation-individuation stage.

It is in this rapproachement subphase that the overall push for autonomy and fear of abandonment reach a crisis. When the mother's own circumstances and needs create an erratic pattern of clinging to and withdrawing from the infant, the normative developmental crisis becomes exacerbated. Often the mother's own separation difficulties in the relationship cause the infant to become a "projective repository" of her own ambivalent needs (Rinsley, 1978). Mahler (1975) observed that problems in this subphase create increased aggression in the child with an alternation between clinging to and repudiating the mother. This may be experienced by the mother as coercive behavior.

This reactive alternating behavior of the child is linked reciprocally to the needs, moods, and circumstances of the mother. When the child moves back toward the mother for "refueling," she may not be there consistently. Situationally, the mother may be preoccupied with other children and related family responsibilities or simply have no available energy. Emotionally, she may be depressed or withdrawn from a nurturing role. These factors may serve to exacerbate the more critical reactive behavior displayed in the mother's anger or disappointment with the infant's movement away from her. At times she either may withdraw, becoming emotionally and physically unavailable, or may cling to the infant, not letting him or her out of her sight or even insisting that the infant sleep with her. Thus, the child learns an inhibiting developmental lesson: he or she cannot have both closeness with *and* separation from the mother.

Kernberg (1975) observed that in the face of this rage toward the mother the infant internalizes an image of being a bad child abandoned by an angry mother. This image is necessary so that the child can cling to the external fantasy of the mother as rewarding and comforting. As the mother retaliates or withdraws from the infant's aggression, the child intensifies these early patterns of splitting and projection.

With the failure to achieve object constancy, the infant continues to experience the world as unpredictable and frightening: "He sees his heroes develop feet of clay as he repeatedly idealizes them and is inevitably disappointed; tiny frustrations assume the dimensions of catastrophes, with ensuing eruption of disproportionately strong affects, often rage" (Carter & Rinsely, 1977, p. 317). Later separations and losses are not worked through as "their counterparts in reality are superficially switched, exchanged or quickly replaced" (Rinsley, 1978, p. 47). The borderline adult-to-be lacks the object constancy to recover from the experience of losing an object. Masterson has characterized this as the inability to mourn: "If one cannot mourn, he becomes fatally vulnerable to object loss" (1976, p. 33).

The Primary Borderline Defenses

As we have discussed, the infant's inability to achieve object constancy leads to weak ego formation. This results in the individual's need to employ some of the more primitive

defensive mechanisms, mainly splitting and projective identification, but also denial, idealization, omnipotence, and
devaluation (Adler, 1972; Kernberg, 1975).

The characteristic defenses in this diagnostic constellation all tend to support and reinforce one another. For example, the individual's denial of aspects of his or her own
emotional experiences reinforces the splitting process and
serves to camouflage potential conflicts. The role of idealization supports the splitting process in its tendency to view objects as totally good or totally bad while reciprocally the splitting itself facilitates both omnipotence and devaluation. Borderline individuals may become grandiose and omnipotently
controlling in their relationships with others. This often
results in devaluation and/or rejection of close objects experienced as threatening or frustrating (Kernberg, 1975).

Thus it is apparent that the defensive patterns identified
with borderline individuals are reciprocally connected.
However, splitting and projective identification comprise the
primary constellation of defenses unique to the borderline
condition.

Splitting

The defensive process of splitting allows the borderline
individual to manage the intolerable ambivalence in
relationships by separating the representation of the objects into "all good" and "all bad" components. This serves
to protect the individual's weak ego structure from inherent
frustrations and contradictions in present and past
relationships. This has been characterized as a preambivalent ego state in which the good and bad aspects of an
object are never integrated internally. Thus, the individual
perceives very few "gray" areas, particularly in relationship
situations.

Kernberg (1975) characterized defensive splitting as a
sharp dissociation between self and object representations.
This results in a reduced capacity to test reality, a low
tolerance for anxiety and frustration, and the inability to
sustain stable and integrated object relationships (Shapiro et
al., 1975). It should be noted here that "good" and "bad"
connote affective states of pleasure and discomfort, not
moral or value judgments (see Kernberg, 1975).

This failure to develop integrated object representations characterizes the borderline individual's relationships by limiting his or her capacity for understanding and empathizing with others in a close relationship (Masterson & Rinsley, 1975). Additionally, the potential for abrupt emotional shifts between these good and bad perceptions of the other person characterize dramatically the borderline individual's mood instability and poor impulse control (Kernberg, 1977).

For example, a borderline individual approaches a close emotional relationship with caution and an intolerance for ambivalence. When the relationship is gratifying, the borderline individual develops positive fantasies and makes the negative fantasies unavailable by splitting them off. When the relationship becomes frustrating, the negative fantasies become abruptly prominent and all memory of the positive aspects of the relationship are unavailable. This illustrates the process of splitting whereby these positively and negatively connotated fantasies move alternatively into and out of consciousness (Shapiro, 1978).

Projective Identification

Projective identification functions to manage unacceptable parts of one's self by projecting them onto another individual in a close relationship. This results in an identification with, or possible reaction to, the reciprocal object who has accepted these projected attributed parts. This defensive pattern is found along a broad range of both normal and abnormal behavior. Its severity is determined by the content of the projection, the individual's capacity to test reality and differentiate from the object, and the need to avoid conflict by disavowing the dystonic aspect of oneself (Shapiro, 1978). Finell (1985) observes that the complexity of projective identification involves individual defenses, modes of relating and communicating, and subtle interpersonal interaction. Depending on the interaction of these factors, projective identification may contribute to either an empathic quality in a relationship or a delusional distortion which binds the relationship (Zinner & Shapiro, 1972).

In simple projection, the projected parts are left with the other person. However, in projective identification the relationship evolves through the efforts of one to induce in the other a collusive conformity to the specific aspects of the projections (Shapiro, 1978). Thus these defensive patterns involve both internal and interactional components.

Projective identification becomes a major mechanism in the borderline individual's need to control the perceived danger in close relationships. The individual will try to evoke behaviors in the other person which confirm the projection while at the same time the object accepts these projected attributes as part of him or herself. Kernberg (1977) has concluded that the weak ego boundaries of the borderline individual prevent the maintenance of simple projection and result in the identification with the object. He has suggested a process whereby the borderline individual continues to experience the projected parts/impulses (even after the projection), fears the object who has accepted the projections, and thus needs to control or attack the object. In such a relationship, the borderline individual disregards the reality of the object which may contradict the projection and, while consciously identifying with the projected disavowed parts in the object, sustains an unconscious vicarious experience with those projected attributes (Shapiro, 1978).

The dramatic elements of projective identification are reported frequently by clinicians in the transferential aspects of psychotherapy with borderline individuals. The borderline individual's inability to integrate positive and negative aspects of the internalized object creates a high sensitivity to minor frustrations in therapy. When these occur, the borderline individual withdraws all affectively positive perceptions of the therapist and, through projective identification, experiences the therapist as "attacking" or "rejecting." The borderline client needs to control defensively the therapist whose image has been distorted by these aggressive projections. This inhibits the therapeutic process and requires the therapist to struggle continuously to maintain a level of reality in the therapeutic alliance (Shapiro et al., 1975).

The borderline individual's continued utilization of projective identification serves to reinforce the inherently weak ego functioning (Shapiro, 1978). The projection of aggressive elements (primitive idealization) also results in the borderline individual's continued dependency, loneliness, and fear of separation (Klein, 1946).

As indicated, the borderline individual possesses an acute sensitivity to underlying threats in a close relationship. Here projective identification becomes highly coercive in that the borderline individual's perceptual accuracy in the projection is usually on target with an area of conflict in the reciprocal object (Shapiro, 1978). This explains the uncanny reciprocal response by the object in accepting the projections, which can often be observed clearly in the reciprocal dynamics of a borderline individual's marital interaction. In individual psychotherapy, the borderline client will use this perceptual targeting to provoke a response by the therapist in such a way as to justify the distrust as well as to devalue the therapist (Adler, 1972).

THE ROLE OF FAMILY THERAPY

This chapter has sought to prepare the reader for the discussions regarding family assessment and treatment in the following chapters. The general hazards and vulnerabilities that any therapist may experience in treating borderline families have been presented initially so that the reader may identify and track his or her own prior clinical experiences through the following chapters. The discussions regarding the problems of individual psychotherapeutic approaches and the review of borderline literature and brief introduction to object relations theory provide a background for the discussions of family assessment dynamics and the role of family therapy that follow.

We have alluded to our approach to family therapy as being "integrative." The reader who is less familiar with the growing literature in the family therapy field may have an image of family therapy that represents only a single orientation, perhaps derived from one book or a certain workshop attended. As recently as four or five years ago, family therapists would greet new acquaintances at conferences with the inevitable question "What kind of family therapy do you do?" The answers would typically identify a particular family therapy pioneer that one had studied with or a training center that taught a certain orientation.

The overall range of co-existing orientations in the family therapy field has been broad and confusing. These orientations are represented, for example, as structural (Minuchin), strategic (Haley, Weakland, Watzlawick, etc.), family of origin (Bowen), psychodynamic/object relations (Ackerman, Framo, etc.), intergenerational (Nagy), existential (Whitaker), and communication (Satir). Therapists entering the family therapy field a decade ago, who studied with a pioneer or training center that represented a singular orientation, tended to view family therapy as being practiced only from their own often narrow orientation. The decade of the 1970s was characterized by a period of considerable competition between these so-called "disciples" of certain pioneers and their second and third generation training centers.

However, the family therapy field has matured dramatically over this past decade and moved significantly toward a more integrative approach. This has been accomplished notably by the extensive development of doctoral and masters level graduate programs offering specific degrees in family therapy. These academic programs have led the way by teaching broader and more integrative approaches to family therapy.

By "integrative," we mean that we begin with a basic systemic understanding of human behavior within an intergenerational family system. To understand the complexity of personal development and behavior within a family system, one must integrate historical/intergenerational/psychodynamic understandings with the interactional resources of structural/strategic/communication theories. Clinical assessment builds intrinsically on these integrated theories while clinical practice evolves from theory and assessment. In the following chapters we will show how such an approach facilitates the understanding and treatment of borderline families.

Chapter 2

Defining the Borderline Family: An Analysis of Transgenerational Data

This chapter will develop a descriptive definition of the borderline family through an analysis of available psychiatric clinical data reported in the literature. These data will be organized and reconceptualized according to what we have defined previously as integrative systemic family theory. This represents a unique approach within the family therapy field in that these clinical observations, which were reported regarding typically only one aspect of borderline dynamics, will be analyzed and blended to make a systemic whole.

Such a process was both necessary and challenging. As we have indicated, there have been very few efforts to relate the borderline condition to marital and family dynamics and patterns. Similarly, *almost all of the observations and clinical data regarding borderline dynamics in the literature have been reported by individually oriented investigators and clinicians based solely on diagnosed borderline individuals.* The challenge for us was to organize these data from a more broadly defined systemic orientation and to identify consistent patterns that had not previously been recognized or integrated from a family systems perspective. This process demonstrated clearly the value of systems theory as an organizing mechanism for what appeared to be random and disparate data. The process of reconceptualizing the interactive and reciprocal dynamics evident from these data led to the identification of consistent clinical patterns. Of course, the reliability of this process is based on the premise that dynamics and interactional patterns within the family system form a powerful matrix of emotions and behaviors. These influences typically flow across generational boundaries, producing clinically predictable phenomena at certain developmental junctures.

FAMILY SYSTEMS PATTERNS IN CLINICAL RESEARCH: AN INTERGENERATIONAL ANALYSIS

As we have indicated, the borderline condition appears to evolve from a milieu of family turmoil and disorganization. The foregoing discussion reviewed the basic theoretical understanding of the etiology and internal dynamics of the borderline individual. This section will organize the available clinical data on borderline patterns from a family systems and intergenerational standpoint that will include parental and spousal family of origin patterns, the mate selection process, and parent-child subsystems. This analysis will take the reader beyond individual dynamics to a recognition of broader interactive and intergenerational patterns which will aid in the identification of systemic etiological patterns and in clinical assessment. This discussion will establish a baseline foundation for the presentation of our own findings, which will be reported in Chapter 3.

The Parental Family of Origin

While there are very few data in the literature regarding the first generation family of origin, there is some concurrence that the parents of diagnosed borderline individuals have themselves experienced separation difficulties from their own families of origin. Shapiro and colleagues (1975) suggested that these parents remained "symbiotically" bound to their own families of origin and carried into their own parenting roles associations either that autonomy is "good" and dependency is "bad" or that autonomy is "bad" and dependency is "good." The parent's self image may be one of a "lovingly dependent" or "strong and autonomous" person. The characteristic alternate to the one perceived would then be projected elsewhere.

Similarly, Mandelbaum (1977) has suggested that these parents of borderline individuals remained "deeply enmeshed" with their own families of origin. He reported that while distance or isolation may be observed in relationships with parents or siblings, these factors do not represent genuine differentiation or autonomy. Walsh (1977) also reported that these first generation parents had experienced their own separation traumas with their families of origin during childhood.

The Family of Origin Spousal Subsystem

A review of the literature regarding the parents of the borderline individual reveals a specific range of disturbances that each brings to their respective spousal and parental roles (Table 2-1). In his early works, Masterson (1972, 1976) suggested that the *mother* of the borderline individual could typically be diagnosed as borderline herself. He believed that the mother's own borderline dynamics caused her to experience high gratification during the infant's symbiotic stage and yet an intolerance to the infant's early separation gestures of curiosity and assertiveness. Thus the mother would be responsive to the infant's clinging but unsupportive when the infant attempted to separate. Masterson and Rinsley (1975) reported: "The child needs the mother's supplies in order to grow; if he grows, however, they are withdrawn from him" (p. 167).

Masterson has subsequently revised his diagnostic view of the borderline individual's mother to include a broader range of potential disorders. He reported that while the range of diagnostic features may vary, the central issue was the mother's emotional unavailability, which could have numerous causes.

Other studies have supported this view of the broader range of maternal disturbances. Wolberg (1952) identified mothers of borderline individuals as displaying a range of

Table 2–1
CHARACTERISTICS OF MOTHERS AND FATHERS
OF BORDERLINE INDIVIDUALS

Mothers
  Obsessive-compulsive (Wolberg)
  Narcissistic (Wolberg)
  Competitive/masculine (Wolberg)
  Paranoid (Wolberg)
  Passive/schizoid (Wolberg)
  Psychotic depressive (Gunderson)
  Borderline (Gunderson, Masterson)
  Schizophrenic (Gunderson)
  Emotionally unavailable (Masterson)
  Preoccupied with own fantasy world (Wolberg)
Fathers
  Absent/emotionally distant (Grinker & Werble)
  Passive-aggressive (Wolberg)
  Hostile/aggressive/controlling (Wolberg)
  Paranoid (Wolberg)
  Psychopathic, mild (Wolberg)
  Depressive (Gunderson)

diagnostic features: obsessive-compulsive, narcissistic, competitive and masculine, paranoid, passive, and schizoid. She suggested that while the mother performed the "duty" of mothering, she was more preoccupied with her own fantasy world. In a study of 12 borderline individuals, Gunderson and colleagues (1980) reported the mothers' diagnoses respectively as depressive with psychotic characteristics (7), borderline (2), schizophrenic (1), and undiagnosed (2).

Mahler (1971) has identified the importance of the *father's* role during the child's normative separation-individuation phase as a "protector" from the potentially overwhelming "mother of separation." The father's failure to perform such a role plays a significant reciprocal role in the emerging family process. Grinker and Werble (1977) observed that the fathers of borderline individuals fail, through their absence or emotional distance, to counteract the regressive pull of the mother, allowing her to gain exclusive control of the infant.

Wolberg (1952) identified four characteristic patterns in these fathers: passive-aggressive; hostile, aggressive, controlling; paranoid; and mildly psychopathic. Gunderson and colleagues (1980) reported finding consistently depressive features in the fathers of borderline individuals.

The *marital relationship of the parents* has received varied evaluations. Gunderson and colleagues (1980) reported a striking absence of overt marital hostility. They described a "rigid tightness" in the marital bond which existed to the exclusion of parental attention, support, and protection of the children. In other words the attachment needs of the parents toward one another or their own parents appeared to take precedence over the needs of the children. Similarly, Walsh (1977) characterized the parental marriages in her study as characterized by overdependence on one another.

Mandelbaum (1977) reported these parental marriages to be "troubled and volatile" which tended to block the development of effective parental leadership within the family. He described the boundaries between the spousal and parental roles as blurred with little identifiable structure. Shapiro and colleagues (1975) noted the pattern of complementary defenses in these parental marriages with a characteristic use of primitive forms of projective identification. Gunderson and colleagues (1980) reported these projective patterns and suggested that they functioned to rid the marriage of unwanted or hostile components via projection onto the children. These observations explain both the nonconflictual quality observed in these marriages and the parents' own lack of involvement with the children.

The Parent-Child Subsystem in the Family of Origin

Behavior within the parent-child subsystem appears to be pivotal in borderline development (Table 2–2). From the review of the prior data it is apparent that parents who have had difficulty with their own separation from their respective families of origin tend to use their children to defend or gratify these ongoing unresolved conflicts (Ritvo, 1975). Similarly, it has been observed that the anxiety from these internalized parental separation conflicts may trigger an exaggerated fear of object loss (Settlage, 1975). Zinner and Shapiro (1972) have suggested that the more parents tend to carry their own tenuous self-object differentiation patterns

Table 2–2
CHARACTERISTICS OF PARENT-CHILD
INTERACTION IN THE FAMILIES OF ORIGIN
OF BORDERLINE INDIVIDUALS

Children overly involved in spousal subsystem (Mandelbaum)
Parents overly involved with children and in sibling subsystem (Mandelbaum)
Parents complain borderline child is too independent (Shapiro)
Parents complain borderline child is too dependent (Shapiro)
Limited nurturance for the pre-borderline child described as parentified caretaker (Walsh)
Parents unable to respond to normative independent behaviors in child (Zinner & Shapiro)
Child anxious over threat of loss of parental love (Zinner & Shapiro)
Adolescent's inability to separate from family (Walsh)

and rely heavily on projective defenses, the more primitive will be the personality organization fostered in their children.

The family of origin parent-child interaction patterns have been characterized by blurred boundaries (Mandelbaum, 1977) where either the children invade or are pulled into the areas of parental functioning or the parents become intrusively involved and invade the boundaries of the children. These diffuse boundaries are indicative of ineffective parental hierarchies within family systems. Singer (1975) described these parenting patterns as "very restrictive policy making, loose policies and very lenient punishing" (p. 435).

Walsh (1977) identified broader parental behaviors as reflecting either underinvolvement or overinvolvement with their children. Underinvolvement was observed to occur more frequently in her study than it did in the report of Gunderson and colleagues (1980). Borderline adults described their parents as distant, remote, aloof, detached, and preoccupied. Many reported feeling neglected, specifically by their mothers. Those individuals living with a single parent mother described her as unreliable, undependable, and erratic. Walsh's subjects from the overinvolved group reported feelings of high dependency on their parents as well as having been controlled and obligated to comply with parental needs. Some reported feeling "special" to their parents but without a sense of being genuinely cared for or understood.

Similar parent-child patterns have been reported occasionally in the literature. Grinker and Werble (1977) analyzed case data on the families of origin of 47 borderline patients. They reported three descriptive typologies: (1) the family is not a mutually protective unit; (2) the family is excessively protective; and (3) family life is marked by denial of problems. The "mutually protective" group occurred most frequently in their population of cases. Similarly, Shapiro et al. (1975) described two parental typologies: (1) parents complaining that the borderline adolescent was "too independent"; and (2) parents complaining that the child was "too dependent." These patterns create the scenario suggested earlier in which parents who perceive themselves as "lovingly dependent" view the developing borderline child as "ruthlessly independent." On the other hand, if the parents perceive themselves as "strong and autonomous," the borderline child will be perceived as "ravenously demanding and aggressively dependent."

The actual role of the children in the parent-child subsystem may vary according to the extent to which their behavior requires attention or support from the parents (Gunderson and colleagues, 1980). Walsh (1977) suggested that the borderline as a child had been perceived by the parents as the "good child," i.e., the one who stops fights, behaves responsibly, and never cries. She described this child's role as the "parentified caretaker." The parents' interaction with this child lacked nurturance even when the borderline child was ill. One such adult borderline subject reported: "If I'm sick, like now, they'll take care of me, but if I'm well I have to take care of my mother, her emotional needs" (p. 168).

It appears that the early development of the prospective borderline individual may be characterized by the parents' inability to respond to the child's normative independent and nurturant needs. The child's resultant anxiety over potential loss of parental love causes the modification of subjective experiences according to the parental projections (Zinner & Shapiro, 1975). In other words, the threat of loss renders the child vulnerable to the projections which occur within the family. This dilemma creates what Shapiro and co-workers (1975) have defined as "developmental interference" and leads to what they describe as "an intensification of negative self and object images and a resultant pathological continuance of defensive splitting of positive and negative internalized relationships" (p. 402).

As the prospective borderline individual proceeds developmentally through childhood, he or she may experience another potential developmental crisis during late adolescent separation. Walsh (1977) reported that 13 out of her 14 adult borderline subjects identified the onset of major symptoms within the year of attempted separation from their families. Most of these subjects chose to return home rather than to continue their painful attempts at being separated. Five of these subjects attempted suicide during this period of separation. (See Carter and Rinsley, 1977; Singer, 1975; Shapiro et al., 1975; and Zinner and Shapiro, 1972, for additional studies which address the treatment of diagnosed borderline adolescents.)

The only available data regarding the sibling subsystem in the family of origin of the borderline individual have suggested that these relationships are full of conflict, with the siblings behaving in a hostile and rejecting manner toward one another (Grinker & Werble, 1977; Walsh, 1977).

AN INTERGENERATIONAL MODEL OF BORDERLINE FAMILY DEVELOPMENT

The data that have been reviewed present glimpses of various aspects of a borderline individual's early development. These were presented to assist the reader in beginning to identify systemic and developmental threads of etiology. The following developmental model is intended to integrate aspects of our own clinical data with that from the literature that has been reviewed.

The model will be presented in the context of intergenerational family theory and represents the identification of etiological threads that lead up to adulthood, including mate selection and family formation (these latter patterns will be analyzed in Chapter 3). We believe that this model is unique in the literature because it provides a systemic family orientation that recognizes developmental etiological patterns in borderline development which span at least four generations, and it identifies unique and consistent structural and interactional characteristics of the family system which will aid in clinical assessment and treatment planning. The various concepts utilized here from systemic family theory and those conceived in this study are defined in the Appendix. This model spans a four-generational developmental process.

As we have indicated, data from our study of over 200 cases spanned nearly 8 years and was collected from a variety of inpatient and outpatient clinical settings. These data are primarily clinical and descriptive in nature, and represent predominantly a Caucasian, middle to upper middle class population. In the early phase of the study, the clinical investigation focused exclusively on families in which an adult parent had been diagnosed as borderline, of whom nearly 90% were the mothers. We believe some skewing occurred in part because of our focus on family cases and parent-child patterns. However, it has been suggested in the literature, and our observations support this, that male borderline individuals have more difficulty with family separation and differentiation than do females. As a result males have more difficulty leaving their families of origin, they more frequently never marry, and they tend to remain more closely tied to their families of origin during their adult lives.

Approximately 40% of our subjects were intact families; the remainder were post divorce single parent families and stepfamilies. As our study progressed, we recognized the existence of structurally identifiable borderline patterns in family systems in which no parent had been previously diagnosed as borderline. At this point we began to include in our study population these more broadly identified borderline systems. These cases sought or were referred to clinical services because of the terrorizing behaviors of the "bad" child or less frequently by depressive symptoms displayed by the "good" child. Children so identified in the study population ranged in age from 7 to 23 years.

It is our belief that borderline development evolves over at least three and perhaps four family generations. The central pattern observed in these family systems is one of multigenerational enmeshing and clear centripetal features. This is supported in the literature by numerous references to the binding aspects of the families and the chronic separation and individuation problems of their members. At all generational levels, despite erratic patterns in parent-child attachment, it appears that members are tightly bound emotionally to their families of origin and that vertical loyalties take precedence over horizontal loyalties.

The process of mate selection and family formation at the second generation, i.e., the parents of the borderline carrier, occurs in a tenuous manner with both prospective spouses clinging to their own enmeshing families of origin. The mate selection process itself appears to be characterized by an emotionally needy, yet dominating female who selects a more passive, dependent, and distant male who will not challenge or threaten her unrelinquished loyalties and vertical ties to her own family of origin. Reciprocally, the male selects such a female partner who with her pseudo-strength can nurture his dependency needs at a distance and also tolerate his own clinging vertical loyalties.

Both partners collude to allow and tolerate each other's continuing and intense family of origin ties as well as to minimize the expected levels of attachment and intimacy with one another in the marriage. This complementarity produces a classic marital interaction pattern that Wynne and coworkers (1958) defined as pseudo-mutuality. The relationship may appear overly dependent on the surface but emotional integration and attachment are lacking. Thus the marital interaction may display an absence of tension with a blurring of marital and parental boundaries.

The wife (and mother of the prospective borderline individual) appears to have had a more fragmented emotional development than the husband. She carries the more observable personal symptomatology ranging from emotional preoccupation and unavailability to alcoholism or even psychoses. The complementarity of this parental marriage sets the stage for a child to be pulled dramatically into the collusive needs of the parents. The father's pseudo-dependency on the marriage and his continuing vertical ties render him both emotionally and physically unavailable to the child, which allows exclusive control by the mother.

The tenuousness of the parents' marital bonding allows the triangulation of the child by the parents to occur early. This triangular relationship pattern functions to maintain a semblance of balance within the system. Typically, the triangulation takes the form of pulling a child into the spousal subsystem, resulting in the child's performing a parentified caretaking role. We have not identified any consistent ordinal position of this parentified child (i.e., the future borderline carrier). The triangulation appears to occur as a result of developmental or situational issues in the family that may push one or both parents into a more intense involvement with their families of origin. For example, this may occur when one of their parents has been hospitalized for a physical incapacitation, alcoholism, or psychosis.

This parentified child, destined to be the borderline carrier, becomes caught in a confusing and erratic emotional web in which his or her independent activities threaten the enmeshing and dependent needs of the parents and his or her dependent needs threaten the parents' own attachment fears and family of origin loyalties. To these factors are added special access to the parents within their spousal boundaries, the power of caretaking and mediating with the parents, and often responsibilities for the siblings and household. For this parentified child, the intensity of the caretaking role may be great at times, particularly when the mother enters into a period of incapacitation. However, the parentified child soon learns that by occupying this "special," though demanding, place within the family system, his or her fears of abandonment become less acute and more manageable.

The special attention and inordinate level of responsiblity gained by this parentified child triggers intense sibling jealousy and rivalry that will carry into adult years. Many borderline carriers as adults report alienation from their siblings, which is a product of this relationship pattern. The reciprocal function of this triangle within the system serves to reinforce the parentification of the child while maintaining an apparent conflict-free marital relationship for the parents.

As this parentified child feels the normative separation pull of late adolescence, the centripetal forces of the family system act in a counterbalancing fashion. By this point in the formation of the system, its interaction and behaviors have organized around the powerful role of a parentified child who has stabilized the marriage and the system and pulled them through many crises. Thus the early efforts by this parentified child to leave home are typically aborted and often associated with suicidal behaviors and other symptom formation. However, the intensity of this separation crisis for the family gradually undermines the power of this child's parentified role. The system itself will begin to react to the child's potential separation as abandonment and the parentified child may fall into disfavor.

It has appeared in our observations that it is easier for female parentified borderline carriers than for males in similar roles to achieve some separation and move into a marital relationship. In Walsh's 1977 study all five of the males in her population had never married. In Grinker and colleagues' study of "excessively protective" families, all six of the borderline males had never married. Theoretically, it would appear that the cross-gender parentified intensity between a male child and the mother inhibits even marginal separation, limits effective male role modeling, and continues the intergenerational enmeshment and blurring of boundaries. Thus the male borderline carrier has great difficulty forming extrafamilial and specifically heterosexual attachments.

The female child appears to manage her separation anxiety, and perhaps guilt, by replicating through mate selection the identical role models from her family of origin. Most such females, while remaining heavily invested in their vertical loyalties, tend to select passive and distant males who are themselves inadequately separated from their own families of origin.

In this developmental and intergenerational systemic model we can see the often dramatic linkage between explicit former and/or continuing family of origin roles and experiences and the resultant adult mate selection patterns (this will be analyzed further in Chapter 3). This process of tracing and analyzing the etiological development of the borderline family illustrates well what Fogarty (1976) has defined as an intergenerational "funneling effect" whereby certain organizational systemic patterns become transposed across several generations, reaching an "apex" when symptoms appear. The intergenerational model we have just developed will be explicated in more detail in the next chapter as we follow the formation of the borderline family in the development of the marital and parent-child subsystems. As we will describe, the specific borderline symptom formation may occur in the third-generation parent as the borderline carrier or it may not appear until it is further transposed through splitting and projective identification into dramatic behaviors of the fourth-generation children of the borderline family system.

Chapter 3

A Clinical Model of the Borderline Family

As we have indicated, the data which form the basis for this work have been collected from over 200 clinical families in a variety of treatment settings over an 8 year period. In this chapter we will present a clinical model of the borderline family which has evolved from these data and is organized around systemic family theory. It is our experience and belief that new theory emerges from the reciprocal interplay between clinical intervention/practice and clinical observation such that the theory serves to organize and inform the evolving structure and process of therapy.

We believe that this systemic model goes far beyond the individual and symptom-oriented literature previously reviewed by virtue of its introduction of interactive and developmental features. This family model will provide for the clinician a broad view of etiological development as it occurs in both the symptomatic individual and the dysfunctional family system as well as a newly defined family organizational typology—namely the borderline family system. This model will also provide the therapist with a clear systemic foundation for the development of clinical strategies (to be discussed in Chapters 4 and 5) that go beyond the approaches of individual psychotherapy. Such broad intergenerational systemic assessment is necessary for the

47

therapist to recognize clinical dynamics which will aid the development of attachment and control in the early stages of family therapy. To operationalize this clinical model, we have selected an illustrative family case that will be highlighted throughout the chapter.

FAMILY FORMATION—MATE SELECTION AND FAMILY OF ORIGIN PATTERNS

The normative process of mate selection is crucial in family assessment because it identifies dramatic clinical phenomena which link both present and past interactional dynamics that define expectations and patterns in the prospective marital relationship. These identifiable factors characterize each prospective mate's potential for integrating former roles and attachments from the family of origin with the new opportunities for intimacy and companionship in the marital relationship. This selection and early attachment process is characterized by the systemic concept of inter-generational loyalties (Boszormenyi–Nagy & Spark, 1973). Mate selection involves balancing vertical loyalties to one's parents and family of origin with the evolving horizontal loyalties to one's prospective marital partner. This establishes for the clinician the dramatic interplay of historical roles and the development of present attachment.

Other major components in the mate selection process include the idealization of the spouse and the relationship and an underlying protective collusion which develops between the prospective mates. These dynamics function to balance each individual's emotional need patterns in a complementary fashion (Winch et al., 1954) and to gain an expectably "safe" relationship in which one's own personal and internal vulnerabilities will be protected (Dicks, 1967).

Thus mate selection represents the culmination of the courtship process of discovery and testing based on what Dicks (1967) has termed "a mutual signalling system" whereby prospective spouses recognize one another to be within a range of acceptable closeness and comfort. This process is both circular and developmental with regard to the historical roles and experiences that each prospective spouse brings to the new relationship. On the one hand, it represents the extension or repetition of roles and models from one's family of origin, and on the other hand, it is an opportunity for new growth through further ego development and the development of close heterosexual attachment.

Within borderline family systems, we have observed clearly distinguishable patterns in the mate selection process. Here both mates have consistently come from emotionally binding and highly enmeshing families of origin. These background factors serve to enhance and reinforce each spouse's respective vertical loyalties as well as diminishing their potential for dyadic bonding and later availability for parenting. The notable variation in this pattern of parallel intergenerational enmeshment was identified in nearly one third of the husbands in the borderline marriages who came from disengaging family of origin systems: these individuals were essentially loners with few family ties (see Lenny's family history in the following case). Nevertheless, their mate selection and marital interaction patterns were similar to those of the highly enmeshed males.

In our observations we noted a critical intergenerational dynamic in that the majority of our population reported that their early attachment with their own parents was often frustrating and unsatisfactory due to their parents' own similarly enmeshing families of origin and resultant limited availability for parenting. In other words, the parents of the spouses in these borderline families had continued to be more involved with their own respective families of origin than with one another or their children.

These factors identify the linkages between the first and second generations in a three-generational pattern of intense family enmeshment. This creates a climate in which the family of origin parents were either emotionally erratic or basically unavailable to the children for nurturing and support. Since each parent in the family of origin continued to be bound up in their own vertical loyalties, bonding within their own marriages was limited. Such parental marriages could often be identified by their characteristic pseudo-mutuality (Wynne et al., 1958)—the appearance of a conflict-free surface alignment in the relationship which covers underlying stress and dissatisfaction. These factors will become clear as we introduce Susan and Lenny's family systems (see Figures 3–1 and 3–2).

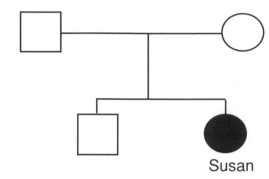

FIGURE 3–1. Susan's Family of Origin

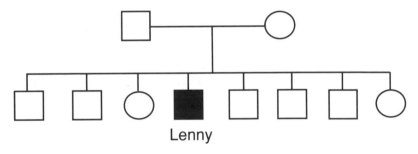

FIGURE 3–2. Lenny's Family of Origin

Susan is a 28-year-old female and the youngest of two children from an enmeshing family. Her older brother was described as the "black sheep" of the family and left home at an early age. Her father, a pharmacist, had difficulties with drug abuse for many years. Her mother was an alcoholic with a history of psychiatric hospitalizations for manic depression. These began as substantial mood swings following her discovery of an extramarital affair involving Susan's father which occurred shortly after Susan's birth. Her family had settled in a retirement community several miles from Susan's mother's parents. Susan was responsible, throughout her years at home, for caring for her father and the household during her mother's hospitalizations. She also cared for her mother during her depressive and occasionally regressive episodes when she would hide for days in her bedroom. Susan dated infrequently during adolescence and remained with the family until she began living with Lenny when she was 23 years of age.

> *Lenny is a 34-year-old male and the fourth eldest of eight siblings. His father was a dominating figure, and his parents' marriage was characterized by conflict and several separations. Family ties were limited and disengaging.* Lenny left home at 17 and began work in several trades, finally becoming a self-employed carpenter, a career he continues to pursue. Although he began college, he dropped out as soon as he was told he was not eligible for ROTC due to visual problems. He has little contact with his family, who live in another city.*

Susan and Lenny both came from families in which the parents were emotionally unavailable and maintained intense vertical loyalties. As a result, neither child experienced sufficient parental bonding due to their parents' emotional unavailability. Susan particularly had to take over many adult tasks in the family during her parents' illnesses. Lenny's disengaging family of origin system represents one of the few exceptions that we have seen to the three-generational patterns of enmeshment. The husbands in borderline families who came from disengaging systems typically "wandered away" or were expelled from their families of origin, often during later adolescence. They separated from their families early, became loners, and maintained few loyalties.

As we reported, in practically all of our study population, the identified borderline adult or the carrier of borderline traits has been the wife. As a child she was often pulled into her parents' spousal subsystem and given excessive caretaking responsibility, often due to the the physical or emotional disabilities of her mother. This pseudo-parental role in the family took the form, both emotionally and often physically, of caretaker for the parents, the siblings, and other extended family members.

We have previously identified this process whereby a child or other individual takes on excessive caretaking duties as *parentification*. In these family of origin systems, this serves to balance reciprocally the parents' unavailability in their nuclear family system due to their own family of origin

---

* While we have reported previously that two thirds of the males in our study were from enmeshing systems, this particular case offers a broader range of illustrative dynamics.

loyalties and enmeshment. This role also provides a substitute caretaker for the system. In the families of origin of the borderline spouses, this role was an explicit response to emotional and physical disabilities of the parents as well as a mechanism to manage the everyday operation of the family.

While some of the literature has described the identified borderline individual's relations with his or her parents as either underinvolved or overinvolved (Grinker & Werble, 1977; Walsh, 1977; Gunderson et al., 1980), our observations suggest that there is actually an alternation between these emotional polarities based on both developmental sequences and external events. In other words, the borderline carrier as a parentified child in the family of origin may at times be overinvolved with one or both parents and at times underinvolved and withdrawn from the parents. By following some of our clinical population in treatment for as long as 4 years, we have observed that similar though less frequent shifts may continue to occur even during adulthood.

This pattern was seen in Susan's family of origin when her caretaking role shifted in intensity between mother and father according to the pattern of her mother's illnesses and hospitalizations. The husbands in our population did not typically play a parentified role in their families of origin. They displayed more passive-dependent roles, regardless of whether they came from enmeshing or disengaging families.

Based on these dynamics, it becomes clinically predictable that the developmental movement of this parentified child toward expectable separation-individuation during later adolescence may evoke a potential family crisis. With the exception of those husbands who came from disengaging systems, both spouses had difficulty separating from their parents and leaving home. The borderline carrier's own separation experience was often characterized by greater interactional drama, aborted runaway efforts, and occasionally, suicidal gestures.

This systemic pattern is consistent with separation difficulties experienced by parentified children in non-borderline families who typically have difficulty differentiating from their family of origin. Stierlin (1973) has characterized this type of family milieu as centripetal (as opposed to centrifugal): emotional forces bind family members and pull them toward the center of the system.

The separation process for the borderline families' spouses was characterized by great intensity, a dramatic quality of desperateness in the child, and rigid binding and reciprocal clinging among family members within the system. It should be noted that this individual is emotionally bound to the powerful enmeshing qualities of the family of origin system itself, as well as to the reinforcement of the parentified role, and not just to the parents. This dynamic may be confusing to the individually oriented therapist or the less experienced family therapist who typically observes interaction between individuals rather than patterns within the broader system.

An important differential factor that we observed with the parentified borderline carrier, as compared to parentified children in other systems, was that as their early efforts toward separation brought them into disfavor with the family, they were consequently threatened with expulsion from the system. The alternate and more typical response by the family to the fears and drama of this separation process follows what is often characterized as a "suicidal myth" in a family system. This is a shared belief within the system which communicates that the family itself, or an individual member, may not survive if any member chooses to leave the family. These systemic responses seem to trigger for the separating adolescent more intense guilt and a dramatic fluctuation of split allegiances, first to the family and then reactively either to a significant romantic relationship outside of the family or to a fantasy of an external lover as "rescuer." Such factors often lead to an impulsive and reactive departure from home. These dynamics account for the high frequency of aborted runaway and suicidal behaviors observed in the borderline carriers during this developmental stage of adolescent separation.

These experiences tend to propel the child out of the family and into an emotionally premature relationship and marriage, frequently without prior courtship experiences. The borderline carrier, now as wife and potential mother, possesses an often angry and typically needy resolve to be a "better" and more effective mother/parent than she had experienced in her family of origin. This tends to reinforce and intensify her continued parentified role as an adult and her need to enmesh others, particularly her children, as a mechanism of emotional control. Yet the inherent vulnerability to failure will always be internally present both in her own maternal role and as a triggering mechanism for reliving the trauma and inadequacy of her family of origin separation experience. It is perhaps this vulnerability that intensifies her continuing loyalty and enmeshment with her own parents and family of origin.

> *Susan never held a job for very long after high school and usually left a job precipitously, either because of difficulties in getting along with her co-workers or because her mother or father required additional caretaking. She got to know Lenny while babysitting for him and his first wife's son, Josh, over a 2-year period.*
>
> *Lenny and his first wife were both 19 when they married. Their son Josh was born the following year. Lenny's first wife was an inconsistent caretaker who never settled into a parental routine. She was severely disabled in an automobile accident when Josh was 2 years old. Her behavior became erratic and emotionally withdrawn. One year later, after 3 years of marriage, Lenny divorced her and was awarded custody of Josh. Although she continued to live in the same community, neither Lenny nor Josh had any contact with her after the divorce.*

The complementarity in the borderline carrier's own mate selection often replicates the complementarity in his or her own parents' marriage through the selection of a typically passive, dependent, and ineffective spouse. In families in which the borderline carrier is the female, the husband becomes attracted to her enmeshing and parentified qualities, ensuring his continued dependent role. By choosing such a mate, he can replicate his own enmeshing family of origin experience or make up for the lack of nurturing in his own background.

However, this husband cannot foresee that the borderline carrier as a future spouse will always regulate the emotional distance in the relationship and, in fact, will not be capable of the emotional closeness he craves nor will she be able to offer him the reliable parenting he may have experienced or wished for in his own family. Thus the borderline carrier can be assured that she can continue safely in a parentified role and maintain emotional control over the relationship. Susan and Lenny illustrate well this type of complementarity.

> *Lenny was a passive, dependent male who had lacked nurturing in his own family of origin and had been unsuccessful in managing the conflict and stress in his first marriage. Susan, as a parentified child, was accustomed to the nurturer role but was unable to manage emotional closeness because of the rejection she experienced in her own family when she attempted emotional bonding with her inadequate parents. Thus Susan tended to precipitate stress as a means of distancing while Lenny found stress intolerable and withdrew emotionally when crises erupted.*

This reciprocal complementarity between the spouses and the intergenerational continuity of these patterns illustrate effectively what has been termed the systemic "funneling effect" (Fogarty, 1976). In this intergenerational transmission process, certain traits are integrated and dramatized as they pass from one generation to another, reaching fruition in later generations at the apex of the funnel. This model demonstrates a truly systemic process of blending and balancing interacting components over several generational systems and stands in contrast to traditionally perceived individual and intrapsychic etiology.

The interactive patterns of these borderline marital relationships within this nuclear system do not exhibit the same pseudo-mutuality that we identified in those of their parents. By contast, these spousal relationships tend to be characterized by circular periods which shift from intense conflict over family control and interaction issues to periods of great distance and emotional unavailability with one another and the family. Here, as in the spouses' families of origin, the boundaries around the spousal subsystem are quite diffuse. This leads to the development of the characteristic splitting and projective identification within the parent-child subsystem.

> *Six months after his divorce from his first wife, Lenny began living with Susan, the former babysitter (see Figure 3–3). Her parents objected strenuously to the relationship, but for Susan, Lenny represented a stable, reliable individual with a*

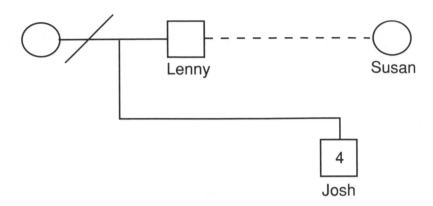

FIGURE 3–3. Lenny and Susan's Premarital System

good job. This was her chance to make the break from the family while retaining a perceived security and close geographical proximity to them. Lenny, at one level, needed a "replacement" mother for Josh, now 4 years old, and Susan already had proven herself in that role as a babysitter. At a deeper level, Susan's presumed caretaking allowed Lenny to continue in a dependent role and offered the hope of receiving the nurturance that he had failed to get from his own parents. Susan moved simply from one caretaking/parentified role to another, and soon she was the dominant figure in the newly formed system. The alienation from her parents lasted for only the first year of their relationship, but it propelled her into an intensive effort to become a "perfect" and all-consuming mother to Josh. Lenny and Susan lived together for 4 years before they decided to marry despite considerable disruptive episodes and conflicts. During the first year of their marriage, their fifth together, Susan legally adopted Josh, assuming that this would solidify her emotional control over both Josh and Lenny. Josh was 8 years old at this time.

SPLITTING AND PROJECTIVE IDENTIFICATION IN THE PARENT-CHILD SUBSYSTEM

The defensive mechanism of *splitting*, as defined previously, is utilized by the borderline carrier to deal with the ambivalence experienced in close relationships which since infancy has been perceived as intolerable. While this unique splitting trait of the borderline carrier may manifest itself throughout a variety of relationship patterns, we have observed that among borderline families, even when no diagnosable individual is present, the splitting phenomenon is still present but diffused throughout the nuclear family system. The content and directionality of the splitting become incorporated into the system's normative functioning and behavior much like other family myths.

Not only does this splitting dynamic pervade the family system but it is operationalized consistently and explicitly within the parent-child subsystem. In this process, positive and negative feelings and thoughts are split apart and experienced by family members in isolation from one another. This splitting distorts the family's perception of reality in such a way as to cause the members to experience both internal and external events and issues as either "right" or "wrong," "black" or "white." The traditional clinical literature has defined this characteristic in individuals as *preambivalence*—the inability to tolerate opposing emotions or perceptions (see Chapter 1). Such rigidly split perceptions occur without regard to the complexities of situations or relationships. In the borderline family system, this process results in a diffusion of internal subsystem boundaries, rigid role assignments for family members, and often closed external family boundaries.

The splitting phenomenon, which occurs in and is experienced throughout the system, supersedes any one individual's role or dynamics. This has been observed elsewhere by Zinner and Shapiro (1972; Shapiro et al., 1975) in their study of the family dynamics of borderline adolescents. They reported that within the family system positive attributes of "goodness" and negative attributes of "badness" are separated and reinvested such that "each family member appears relatively preambivalent and single-minded in relation to the troubled adolescent" (1975, p. 79). They also observed: "Individual members . . . act as if they were the very unidimensional, unconflicted, preambivalent objects that their borderline adolescents perceive them to be" (1975, p. 104).

The function of splitting within the borderline system appears to be the protection of the family from threatening feelings of loss and disappointment as well as from the nega-

tive affects of anger and hostility. These fears and vulnerabilities are carried in varying degrees by the parents
from their respective families of origin directly into the family
formation stage. They then become diffused throughout the
expanding family system with the arrival of children and the
expansion of new subsystems. Splitting produces a shared
or collusive belief and mythology, with both conscious and
unconscious components, which can be observed consistently within the borderline families. The message is that if
such intense affects or feelings were to gain free expression,
the family itself would not survive. Individual family members typically fear becoming overwhelmed, engulfed, or
abandoned, or perceive the potential for violence. These
beliefs become a part of a pervasive family mythology (to be
discussed later) which is shared intrinsically by all members
of the system.

We have identified *projective identification* (see Chapter
2), a concept taken from the traditional literature, as occurring when good and bad aspects of an individual have not
been internalized successfully, resulting in a process
whereby the unacceptable or unpleasant parts of that individual can be denied by projecting them onto an external
object, typically another individual in a close relationship.
The other person, or object, in this process "accepts"
reciprocally the projection and behaves accordingly. This
projective identification phenomenon has been identified also
in the family therapy literature: it was a component of the
"parentification" process as defined by Boszormenyi-Nagy
and Spark (1973); Framo (1972) identified a similar concept
of "irrational role assignments"; Dicks (1967) saw it as a
component of marital complementarity; Bowen (1965, 1971,
1976) defined a "family projection process"; and Skynner
(1981) identified "projective systems."

Our clinical data have allowed us to reconceptualize
projective identification as it occurs within the borderline
family system. It evolves in concert with the systemic splitting process that we have already defined. This projective
process develops rigid role assignments and expectations
among family members, a diffusion of personal boundaries,
and the unavailability and deflection of emotional resources
from one subsystem to another. Family members play out
certain defined roles with one another while remaining vul-

nerable to the intrusive influences or actions of another member. In a spousal relationship, where increasing conflict between the partners may threaten the survival of the system, the conflict, perhaps in the form of aggression, will be projected onto a child. This process affects the system in two ways: first, it protects the spousal subsystem from having to deal with the conflict; and second, it frees the spouses from ever having to work through or accept the conflict as a part of their relationship. For example, as the child "owns" the projection and behaves more aggressively, the spousal subsystem returns to a level of more stable interaction and remains intact. (This process was characterized more generally in the classic description of a scapegoated child; see Vogel & Bell, 1960).

> *Early in their relationship, Susan developed an intense competition with Josh, alternately becoming over-indulgent with him and then moody and demanding, particularly if Lenny spent too much time alone with him. Susan would often take out her frustration with Lenny on Josh, projecting her anger onto him and seeing Josh as "just like his father," i.e., ungrateful and demanding. On occasions Susan would kick Josh and curse at him, seeing him as responsible for their marital difficulties. Eventually Josh became more aggressive himself and increasingly unmanageable. Thus Susan and Lenny successfully deflected much of their own conflict away from the marriage by way of the projective process and through Susan's behavior toward Josh.*

As seen in this case example, the phenomena of splitting and projective identification pervade the borderline family system and become most dramatically operationalized within the parent-child subsystem. The borderline family represents typically a third generation of enmeshment in which the internal differentiation between the subsystems is diffuse, the parents are inadequately separated from their families of origin and maintain continuing high levels of vertical loyalties, and the children are pulled out of their sibling subsystem and into the spousal subsystem to balance the emotional needs of both the marriage and the family system.

We have reported that the emotional life of borderline families revolves around the inability to handle anger and fear of loss and separation. These influences, coupled with the parents' own continuing vertical attachments, create a systemic vacuum or imbalance within the nuclear unit which requires the children to perform rigidly specified roles in the structural organization of the family. These factors contribute to the highly charged and unstable family milieu.

> *During the first year of their marriage, Susan found that Lenny was less available to be "parented" by her and in fact often pulled away from her emotionally and physically. Increasingly, Lenny began to spend more time with Josh than with Susan. Thus, in a competitive maneuver, she focused her energy on winning Josh over to her "side." She idealized him, indulged him, and spent every minute of the day with him. Lenny was being pushed out of the relationship by Susan's behavior, which lasted until Josh entered kindergarten. To Susan's surprise, Josh flourished with his new friends at school and she began to feel increasingly rejected. Her continued efforts to alternately cling to Josh while competing with Lenny for dominance over him began to show in Josh's increasingly resistant behavior. By the time Josh entered first grade Susan had become punitive and easily frustrated with him. She called him unmanageable and ungrateful. She returned now to spending excessive time in her parents' household caring for her mother. At the same time she became increasingly jealous of Lenny's time with Josh.*

In this rigid borderline system, Josh had no alternative but to accept Susan's projected image of him as bad and ungrateful and to become progressively mistrustful of her efforts to nurture him. For Josh, the price of closeness with Susan was both the loss of contact with his father and Susan's complete dominance over him. Due to the splitting phenomenon, the system did not allow for Josh to have both good and bad traits. Thus, he became the bad object for the mother and eventually for the father, too.

COEXISTING TRIANGLES

In general, triangles within a family system are viewed as normative relational building blocks. The three corners or components of triangular relationships offer a central stability amid the array of dyadic relational patterns and alliances within a family system. In the formation of a triangle, a third member is pulled into a dyadic relationship to offer balance and particularly to diffuse stress in the midst of dyadic conflict. This third member is often viewed as the regulator of closeness and distance for the original dyadic component of the triangle (Bowen, 1978). For example, when conflict or stress become problematic in a marital relationship, a child may be typically "triangled in" to the spousal subsystem to serve as either a mediator (parentification) or recipient (scapegoat) of the stress. This process serves to return the marital dyad and the system in general to a stable balance.

While numerous triangular patterns may exist throughout a family system, it is generally expected that each nuclear system will contain an identifiable "central" triangle (see Nichols & Everett, 1986). This means simply that one triangle serves a central balancing function for the entire system and other secondary triangles revolve around this central one. An exception to this typical pattern of one central triangle occurs often in large nuclear systems with seven or more members. Here two central triangles are often necessary to maintain a satisfactory balance due to the size of the system. The reader should understand that triangles are not necessarily dysfunctional; they can serve a constructive and balancing function for all family systems. They represent a central assessment feature for the family therapist.

In borderline families, unlike this typical pattern of one central triangle, our observations have identified a consistent pattern of *two* central triangles. We have termed these *coexisting triangles*. It appears that the unique level of emotional intensity in the borderline family, which we have described, requires the evolution of multiple central triangles. These appear necessary to balance and stabilize the extraordinary features of the borderline system.

These coexisting triangles evolve directly from the splitting and projective dynamics. They typically take the form of split and projected images of a "good" child and a "bad" child within the system. The children "accept" these roles and behave in such a manner as to exemplify these roles both within and without the borderline family. In other words, the borderline system organizes itself around these two central coexisting triangles which typically involve two children. It is our belief that the tenuousness of the parents' marital bonding and the constant underlying threat of destructive anger require *both* identified children to perform such roles in order to dissipate these threats and ensure the survival of the system.

> *One day in the second year of their marriage, Susan came home from her mother's house and announced to Lenny that she was pregnant. They had decided previously not to have children until Susan had been employed for several years so that they would be more secure financially. Lenny believed that Susan was taking a contraceptive pill, which in fact she had discontinued secretly 6 months earlier. This was several months after Josh had entered first grade. Susan was elated. She spoke of having the "ideal" child and ignored Lenny's disapproval. Lenny was angry at the deception and withdrew from the relationship until after their child Amy was born. Shortly after Susan and Amy returned home from the hospital, Susan announced: "Now I have someone for myself who cares for me in the family." The birth was followed by a period of sexual dysfunction (dyspareunia) which lasted more than a year and which heightened the emotional distance in the marriage. These circumstances increased Susan's dramatic possessiveness of Amy and the exclusion of Lenny from almost all child care activities (see Figure 3–4).*

Through the event of conception Susan cleverly created an ally for herself within the family. The child became Susan's "good" object and thus evolved the second central or coexisting triangle in this borderline system. Josh had already been cast as the third member and "bad" object of the initial parent-child triangle. If this child and the resultant triangle had not been created, it appeared likely that the potential destructive intensity of the marital conflict would have destroyed the relationship and the system since the existence of only one triangle with a scapegoated child was not sufficiently powerful to deflect the conflict.

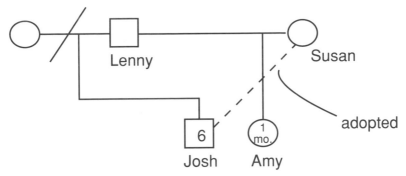

FIGURE 3–4. Lenny's and Susan's Nuclear System After Two Years of Marriage

THE OMNIPOTENT/PSEUDO-PARENTIFIED CHILD

Children who are triangled into the spousal subsystem and assume excessive caretaker roles for either parents or siblings or the family in general have been termed "parentified." Such a child often sacrifices his or her own childhood peer and play experiences to maintain and protect the system. These children typically play the role of the responsible, obedient, "good," nurturing family member and rarely act out or disrupt the system except in desperate efforts to escape. Early in our study, we had assumed that the "good" child in the borderline family was simply parentified. Every clinical family in our population had a "good" child who was either still at home or who had reached 18 to 20 years of age and was living out of the household but nearby. However, as we studied further clinical data, we observed a more complex phenomenon than what is recognized typically as a parentified child. As a result, we have redefined this role as that of the *omnipotent/pseudo-parentified child.*

This "good" child's role, which is triangled into one of the coexisting triangles in the borderline family, supercedes or appears greater than reality. The child is perceived as doing no wrong, he or she follows no rules, acts without consequences, and is unconditionally reinforced. Eventually this child becomes highly manipulative and embodies an anchor point for stabilizing the rest of the family system. The emotional reinforcement from the family collectively for this child in this role is great. As a result, the attention and power of the child within the system trigger a high level of rivalry within the sibling subsystem because other brothers and sisters do not have the same access to the power of the spousal subsystem.

However, this child does not perform a truly nurturing or caretaking role as would be expected of a typically parentified child. In the majority of the borderline families that we studied, *this nurturer/caretaker role was maintained and regulated clearly by a parent and specifically by the borderline carrier* in cases where one was identified. Unlike the typical parentified child that we have described, this child does act out but in primarily covert and manipulative ways. However, such behavior is never punished. In one such case, this omnipotent child was a married, 23-year-old daughter who had been through three abortions before she was 17. She continued to be idealized by the family, who gave her a large formal wedding at 19. She lived four blocks from the family and came to her parents' home every weekday morning before work to have coffee with her mother.

THE PERSECUTING CHILD

The differential pattern of triangulation observed in general family systems, in contrast to that of parentification, involves the "scapegoating" of a specific member, typically a child (see Vogel & Bell, 1960). The child is pulled into the spousal subsystem to dissipate marital stress and conflict. The child accepts these displaced emotions in a projective identification manner, thus becoming the repository for the parents' and family's angry impulses. The scapegoated child typically acts out this stress away from the spousal dyad and usually external to the family system—for example, in delinquent behavior.

Based on our observations, this triangulated "bad" child in the borderline family system represents a special type of scapegoat. He or she accepts the projected anger and conflict as does a typical scapegoat, but instead of simply acting out in delinquent activities outside of the system, this child explicitly turns the anger back onto the family system itself in a persecuting and often terrorizing manner. The behavior displayed by this child may involve physical harm or material destructiveness as well as terrorizing of family members. In one dramatic illustrative case, a persecuting child so terrorized the mother and his "omnipotent" brother when the father was out of town on business that they would lock themselves in a bedroom for hours a night. This pattern had recurred consistently over a 3-year period before the family sought therapy.

To further describe this circular pattern of dynamics for the persecuting child in the system, we have defined a *three-generational persecutory loop* (see Figure 3–5). We identified previously the manner in which anger was not tolerated or dealt with in the parents' own families of origin, which was evidenced in the pseudo-mutuality of their parents' marriages. Anger was experienced by the borderline spouses as

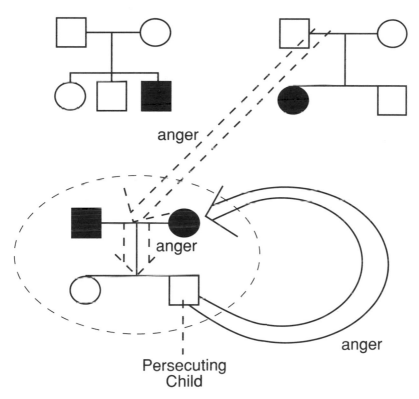

FIGURE 3–5. Three Generational Persecutory Loop

uncomfortable and unacceptable in their own relationship due to its potential destructiveness and threat of loss. Since the anger is not "owned" by either the first or second generations, it is projected onto a member of the third generation (typically a child) through the previously described intergenerational "funneling" effect.

However, due to the highly enmeshing quality of the borderline system and the shared underlying fear of separation and loss, the third-generation "bad" child does not simply act out away from the family but redirects the anger back toward the family system itself. This serves both to dissipate the marital stress and to reinforce the split-off and projective nature of the anger within the system. However, this persecuting role also functions clinically to keep the child closely enmeshed with the family while avoiding the threat of separation and containing the anger at a distance just outside of the spousal subsystem.

As we have indicated, in many clinical families that we have now identified typologically as borderline systems, the borderline carrier may never be identified as the presenting problem for therapy or even diagnosed as borderline. In these families it is often the dramatic persecuting and terrorizing behavior of the "bad" child which is cited as needing treatment. We have hypothesized, based on our observations, that *the greater the degree of persecutory behavior by the "bad" child in the family system, the more intense the therapist can expect the level of deflected spousal hostility to be.* Similarly, *the greater the level of idealization of the "good" child in the system, the greater will be the emotional distance between the spouses.*

> Lenny had soon accepted his new daughter Amy and begun to enjoy a developing relationship with her. However, Susan persisted in clinging tenaciously to Amy. On one occasion, when Lenny wanted to take Amy on a day-long trip to allow Susan to have some private time to sleep, Susan grabbed the child and retreated to a far corner of the shower in the bathroom saying: "How can you take her from me, do you want to kill me too?" Lenny also tried to take a more active parental role with Josh, who was now displaying considerable school and behavior problems, but Susan continued to ridicule his permissiveness with Josh and tried to control

their relationship with her continued angry attacks on Josh. On the occasions when Lenny attempted to intervene, he too became the recipient of Susan's rage. Finally Lenny agreed that Josh was "uncontrollable" and took him to a therapist. Soon after this, when Josh was 11, his anger turned back on the family through verbal and occasionally physical confrontations with Susan. Although Lenny made some attempts to mediate these conflicts, his interventions were weak and ineffectual. He withdrew eventually or simply sided with Susan against Josh.

The respective omnipotent and persecuting roles of children in the borderline system become supported by all of the family members and collusively adopted into the mythology of the family. Once established, these roles become rigid and endure throughout childhood and even after the children have left home and married. These identified children, both the omnipotent and the persecuting, have intense difficulty with separation from the family system as did their parents. Most remain close geographically to the family home and continue patterns in their adult lives as extensions of these dramatic childhood roles.

In support of our theoretical construct of co-existing triangles, it should be noted that among our population of clinical families nearly 70 per cent had two or more children; very few had only one child. In these cases, the single child typically played the role of the "good" child and the father consistently became the "bad" object in the system. In the family systems with sibling subsystems larger than two, we observed that the projected "good" and "bad" roles were consistent and fixed with specifically selected children over time. These roles did not appear to rotate or to be shared.

Occasionally the "excess" children would leave the family prematurely. It often appeared as if they were expelled by the intense exclusivity of the two-triangle system. In only a few systems we observed did these two roles alternate between children or pass from one child to another over a period of years. In the two-child systems, if a child was removed from the family or simply grew up and moved out, the bad object role was shifted to the father. Here the co-existing triangles occasionally overlapped, with one scapegoating the father and the other parentifying the remaining child.

We have theorized that the projections to the "good" child were more critical to the stability of the system since this role tended to remain with the same child over time. Where there was fluctuation, it occurred in the assignment of the "bad" role, which typically shifted to the father when a child was unavailable. It appeared from our observations that the mother/wife as borderline carrier could not tolerate even the pseudo-nurturance of another adult, i.e., the father/husband, in a "good" object role. Thus clinically this "good" child role appeared more rigidly defined.

CLINICAL THEMES OR MYTHS AND SYSTEMS TYPOLOGIES

Family Themes or Myths

Most family systems tend to display clinical themes or myths which characterize how members of the family view themselves and their relationship to the external world. These themes or myths represent powerful group perceptions which may spread throughout several generations and control both the internal and external behavior of the members. Other clinicians working with diagnosed borderline individuals have observed that the typical symptomatology of the diagnosed borderline individual is not limited to that person but is shared and acted upon by all members of the family system. Mandelbaum (1980) has suggested that the borderline individual's symptoms became a "ritualized part of family life," and serve to maintain the homeostasis of the system. Similarly, Zinner and Shapiro (1972) reported a group phenomenon of shared splitting within families of diagnosed borderline adolescents.

In our observation of borderline families we have identified consistently two central clinical themes: (1) "negative feelings are destructive"; and (2) "loss and separation (physical or emotional) are intolerable." These themes permeate the entire nuclear system and arise clearly from the intensity of emotional needs and the splitting and projective process in the system. The family system must accommodate such that the roles of the omnipotent and persecuting children serve to confirm these themes and offer balance to the system. In

other words, these themes function in a systemically collusive manner such that certain roles are performed and
maintained for the good (survival) of the system itself.

The family's concern that negative feelings are destructive can be traced to the borderline parents' respective
families of origin and represents a belief embedded in the
make-up of the three-generational system and its members.
However, this does not mean that negative feelings are not
expressed in borderline families. To the contrary, borderline
families often experience periods of intense rage and impulsive anger. These intense displays serve to confirm the
potential danger of angry feelings. Thus, the anger is split off
or kept at arm's length from the system. It becomes projected onto the "bad" or persecuting child who carries the
aggression for the entire system, yet through the persecutory
feedback loop reminds the family of its ever-present danger
and potency.

Reciprocally the role of the "good" child allows the family
to maintain a belief that the system is operating "normally."
The parents will often report to a therapist that they cannot
be accused of providing a destructive environment for their
members since they have raised such a good and perfect
child. In this manner the parents can justify maintenance of
the ongoing system (homeostasis) and resist therapeutic efforts directed toward the whole family. In other words, the
"good" child represents the parents' denial of their own
destructive impulses, and requests for therapy will often
focus on the "bad" child or the symptomatology of the borderline carrier.

Similarly, the borderline family's fear of separation/loss
is often an expression of the parents' own inadequate early
separation experiences. These become intensified in their
own nuclear system by the presence of children and evolve a
multi-generational pattern of high enmeshment and blurred
or diffuse boundaries. However, this does not mean that
there is actual emotional closeness or intimacy in the borderline system. In fact, in contrast to a typical enmeshing
family, there is considerable emotional distance, which is
regulated and determined by two factors: (1) the degree of
each parent's vertical loyalties; and (2) the relative rigidity of
the children's projected roles. It is critical for the therapist to
understand that the borderline family does not appear to be

able to mourn losses or to accommodate readily to the movement of a member away from the family system. This is perhaps because of the tenuous and precarious emotional balance that exists within the system and the fear that the system would become either overwhelming or lost should this balance be upset.

These patterns have a number of ramifications for the borderline system. For example, the death of a member which occurs anywhere in the multi-generational family system may create explosive repercussions of depression, suicidal attempts, or acting out at various locations in the system. Diagnosed borderline females tend to leave their families of origin with reluctance and are often viewed as "traitors" by their family of origin. Diagnosed borderline males frequently never marry. Many diagnosed borderline adolescents and young adults resort to runaway and suicidal behaviors in dramatic efforts to separate from the family system.

> *Entering their sixth year of marriage, Lenny and Susan had become a family with a rebellious and confrontative adolescent (Josh) and an indulged and spoiled kindergarten-aged child (Amy) who was reluctant to be left at school. Their marital relationship had become distant though stable. However, their lives changed dramatically when Susan's mother killed herself with a gunshot to the head (see Figure 3–6). Susan's behavior became erratic, ranging from sullenness to explosive rage. She alternated between clinging to Amy and then spending weeks at a time away from Lenny and the children comforting and taking care of her widowed father. This dramatic shift in behavior created an expectable imbalance in the system which allowed Lenny to assume a more direct parental role with both children. He was able to display caretaking and playful resources with the children that had never before been present within this system. Eight months after her mother's suicide, Susan's efforts to return to control in the family system were rebuffed. The system had changed. Lenny now had control of the parenting, the children were responding well to him, and the projected roles had begun to lose their power. The marriage became progressively more volatile. There were several stormy separations during which Susan moved back with her father. Finally, Susan*

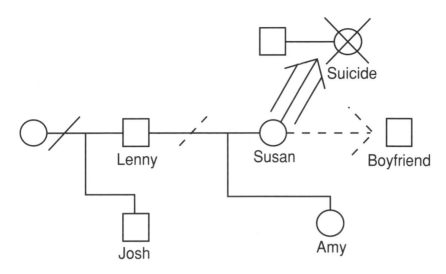

FIGURE 3–6. Lenny and Susan's Post-Separation System

abruptly took Amy from Lenny, claimed that Josh was not her son and that she wanted nothing to do with him, and moved in with an unemployed, transient male. This set the stage for a bitter and lengthy custody battle.

In Susan and Lenny's marriage, the dramatic, though not unpredictable, suicide of Susan's mother created a systemic imbalance to which the fragile three-generational system could not accommodate successfully. Susan's vertical loyalties to her father, based on early developmental deficits as the borderline carrier, became intensified and diminished her loyalties to her spouse and children. Unable to effectively mourn the loss of her mother, Susan became less available emotionally to her own children, which made it possible for Lenny to become more dominant in the system and effective as a parent. Susan experienced this as a threat to her possessive need of Amy and precipitously left the marriage, refusing Lenny access to Amy completely.

Family Typologies

There are few consistent efforts in the literature to define a differential range of borderline family system traits or pat terns. Beavers and Voeller (1983) defined a "borderline" range of traits on a five-part family typology model. Each of the types, i.e., severely disturbed, borderline, midrange, adequate, optimal, are characterized according to centripetal and centrifugal patterns. The borderline centripetal family is described as possessing more internal emotional control such that certain family rules are followed to contain outward expressions of rage or rebellion. In these systems, control struggles are more covert and conflict more verbal than behavioral. The borderline centrifugal family displays more open anger and conflict with a poor parental coalition. It should be noted that Beaver and Voeller's typology represents the family of origin system and not the borderline nuclear system which we have explicated.

The purpose of identifying a clinical typology is to enhance clinical assessment and treatment methods, which will be discussed in Chapter 4. To aid in this process, we have chosen to characterize the borderline systems according to their relative degree of *structural flexibility. Low* structural flexibility in a system is evident when the projected roles of the children are rigid and set, the parents are intensely tied to their own families of origin, and the external boundaries around the nuclear or multi-generational system are rigidly closed and isolate the family from external input. This latter is evidenced by a limited social network. *High* structural flexibility is evident when the system adapts more readily to parental movement between nuclear and family of origin systems. It displays less intensity both in family of origin loyalties and in the enactment of the projected roles of the children. These systems have more permeable external boundaries and greater social contact outside of the family. Individual members of subsystems of these latter families will display less adherence to the themes/myths when they are interviewed individually by a therapist. They will also display more normal social and school functioning.

In terms of differential clinical assessment, these high structurally flexible families may, in the initial interview, appear more dysfunctional and rigid as a result of the system's reactive accommodation to whatever crisis or stress precipitated the clinical referral. The clinician must be careful not to assume prematurely that these families are less adaptable and thus fail to mobilize the interactive resources

that they do possess. Similarly, in an early interview with a
low structurally flexible family, the clinician must be careful
not to incorrectly assess them as more functional or adaptable than they are. This is a common assessment error because the identified client, e.g., the persecuting child, may
effectively contain and display the systemic stress so that
the remainder of the family appears quite calm and functional. Differential treatment strategies will be discussed in
the following chapter. Susan and Lenny's case is one of low
structural flexibility.

> *In the first round of custody litigation between Susan and
> Lenny two therapists recommended in favor of the father for
> custody of Amy. However, the court awarded Susan custody of
> Amy with "liberal" visitation to Lenny. As the therapists
> predicted, Susan repeatedly withheld visitation of Amy to
> Lenny, and when Lenny retained another attorney to intervene
> Susan disappeared with Amy and her boyfriend for nearly 10
> weeks. Lenny had no contact with Amy during this period.
> Amy's behavior became regressive and her social skills
> deteriorated. In addition, she witnessed several knife fights
> between her mother and the boyfriend. On one occasion she
> had intervened to try to protect her mother. During the next
> round of litigation, the father was awarded custody of Amy.
> Susan never appeared in court at the hearing due to
> hospitalization following two suicidal gestures the week
> before the court date. Lenny later married a school teacher
> who had a son from a prior marriage (see Figure 3–7). They*

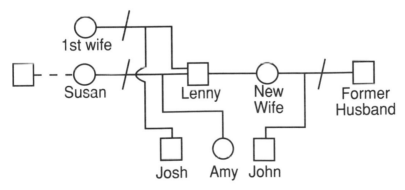

FIGURE 3–7. Lenny's Remarried Stepfamily System

continued in family therapy with one of the authors for 6 months, working toward containing Josh's anger, which was now directed toward the new stepmother. Amy adjusted well to the stepmother and has had limited contact with Susan.

This case of Susan and Lenny has been presented to describe and to operationalize the systemic components we have identified in this clinical model of the borderline family. While idiosyncratic features are present, the history and development of this system are consistent with the transgenerational model of family of origin patterns, mate selection, and spousal subsystem formation. The systemic features of splitting and projective identification are seen clearly in the pseudo-parentified and persecuting roles of Amy and Josh, respectively. Their differential roles within the parental subsystem demonstrate the presence of coexisting triangles, as does Josh's continued disruptive behavior through the persecutory loop even after the marriage had ended. The following chapter will build upon the features of this clinical model through the identification and discussion of explicit family therapy strategies.

Chapter 4

Treating the Borderline Family

We have indicated previously that clinical theory, assessment, and the outcome of practice are inseparably interwoven. This chapter builds upon the clinical model and assessment features of the borderline family and suggests specific patterns of clinical intervention and case management.

FAMILY THERAPY STRATEGIES

It is our experience and belief that successful outcomes of family therapy are the result of careful clinical assessment of the broad family system. The clinician's ability to recognize the complexity of a system's particular structure and process dimensions will inform him or her in the choice of treatment methods and the definition of goals. To move directly into treatment issues, we believe that the following specific clinical goals are relevant for conducting family therapy with borderline families:

1. To increase the family's interactive and perceptive abilities for accepting one another within the system and recognizing that aspects of their relationships and the external world contain both "good" and "bad" features. This involves the clinical task of decreasing the systemic splitting process.

2. To increase the abilities of all family members to "own" or accept potentially negative aspects of themselves and thus to be able to move toward interacting as "whole" persons with one another. This involves the clinical task of "working through" the interpersonal distortions and reducing the systemic projective process.
3. To move the interactional patterns and experiences within the system to a more openly affiliative level. The clinical task here is to reduce the oppositional and stereotypical role behavior of all of the members, particularly that of the persecuting and pseudo-parentified children.
4. To "reset" external boundaries for both the nuclear and intergenerational systems by "closing" the external boundaries around the nuclear system, which will have the effect of reducing the vertical family of origin loyalties for both parents (Fig. 4–1).
5. To "reset" the internal nuclear boundaries for each of the three subsystems, i.e., spousal, parent-child, and sibling. This involves the clinical task of "closing" the internal boundaries between the spousal and sibling subsystems to limit the reciprocal intrusiveness of children and parents into each other's lives. This clinical process will also result in a more clearly defined alliance between the two parents (Fig. 4–2).

Based on our collective clinical experience with these borderline families, we have identified five family therapy treatment strategies (Table 4–1). The clinical implementation of these clinical strategies will be illustrated through the use of an ongoing case, as in the prior chapter.

Jim and Mary Singleton were referred to family therapy with the presenting problem of their 16-year-old son, Billy, who had begun to display threatening behavior toward family members and had been using drugs for several years (see Figure 4–3). He had been discharged from a residential drug treatment program 4 months prior to their entrance into therapy. Billy's problem behaviors were reported to have begun when he was 9 years old, at which time he became increasingly disrespectful toward family members. However, he

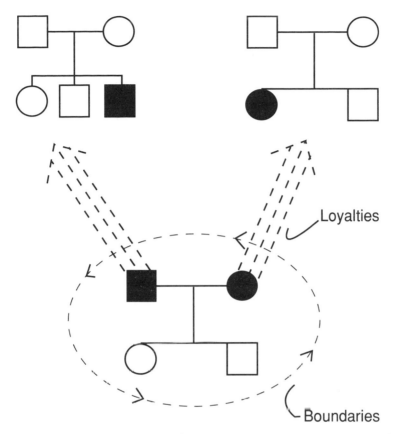

FIGURE 4–1. Closing External System Boundaries to Reduce Family of Origin Loyalties

Table 4–1
FAMILY THERAPY STRATEGIES FOR
BORDERLINE INDIVIDUALS

1. Developing and maintaining a therapeutic structure
2. Reality testing with the family
3. Interactional disengagement
4. Working with the intergenerational system
5. Solidification of the marital alliance and the sibling subsystem

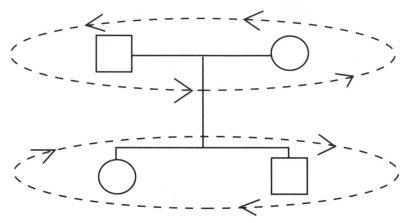

FIGURE 4–2. Closing Internal Subsystem Boundaries

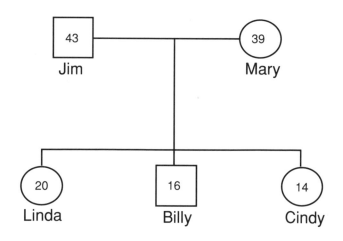

FIGURE 4–3. The Singleton Nuclear System

did not present a problem at school. His parents and two sis-
ters saw themselves as victimized and persecuted by Billy.
Jim, the father, declared that he no longer knew what to do
about his son's behavior. Earlier in the year, he and Billy had
engaged in a physical fight and Billy's rage and lack of con-
trol terrified him. Since that experience Jim had withdrawn
from Billy and the rest of the family, spending more time
away at his work. Mary, the mother, felt abandoned by her
husband in dealing with Billy and was at her "wit's end." She
was advocating "kicking him out of the house." Jim did not
want to resort to such a drastic step.

DEVELOPING AND MAINTAINING A
THERAPEUTIC STRUCTURE

It has been our consistent observation that the typical
characteristics of borderline family systems, i.e., distrust,
fear of abandonment, and impulsivity, are present to potentially sabotage therapy before it has even begun. Whatever
event or crisis has brought the family or identified member
to therapy represents a state of imbalance within the family
system. This results in greater sensitivity and caution in
regard to external influences and a clear "closing" of the system's external boundaries not only to the therapist but to
other outside resources as well. The family therapist's initial
contact with the system often serves to escalate dramatically
the emotional intensity and apparent chaos within the system. Similarly, efforts by the therapist to "enter" or "join" the
system are typically met by resistance; and occasionally, if
the therapist is not sensitive to the system's vulnerability,
the family will simply flee from therapy.

The initial clinical goal of the family therapist is to evolve
carefully a "therapeutic structure" that will be experienced
as "safe" by the family. The use of "therapeutic structure"
here instead of "therapeutic alliance" is intentional because
it defines better the task of engaging the entire family system
rather than simply individuals. The concept of a therapeutic
alliance refers more traditionally to an agreement between
two individuals, i.e., the therapist and the client. The
development of a therapeutic structure defines more accurately a similar process but different task, whereby the

family therapist engages and organizes a structure to treat the entire family system. It is this therapeutic structure that provides a controlled setting and safe milieu for the family. This element of safety must be identified early by the therapist: it is a critical prerequisite to establishing trust in working with borderline families.

The specific dimensions of *establishing* a clear and firm structure are quite pragmatic and often overlooked by even experienced therapists. This begins with reaching an explicit agreement in the initial session with regard to the time, day, and frequency of appointments. These provide an important spatial structure and require consistency by both the family and the therapist. Next the therapist must be clear about setting fees and the management and consequences of cancellations and missed appointments. The therapist must also clearly identify who is expected to attend each session.

The identification and management of these issues should be done in the initial session in a supportive rather than a demanding or officious manner. These are the first steps in defining outwardly for the family an expectable and clear structure, and more covertly a pattern of control by the therapist in at least these relatively non-sensitive areas. As we discussed in Chapter 1, the role of the therapist in establishing control becomes crucial at this early stage. The therapist who has difficulty setting limits or who is more comfortable with a "passive" style will have great difficulty moving farther into therapy with borderline families.

After these initial steps, the therapist must begin to set clear and explicit rules of conduct for the therapy sessions. These are directed toward providing for the physical and emotional safety of family members both within the therapist's office and after they return home. Most therapists tend to manage safety issues as they arise in the course of therapy. However, with borderline families, safety issues must be anticipated and rules set at the beginning of therapy in order to build a working therapeutic structure. These rules are necessary to manage the typical impulsivity of borderline families and the occasional eruption of violence. The rules must be clear and state that threats, intimidation, or violence will not be tolerated in the therapy setting. The typical consequence is that the person or persons involved will be asked to leave immediately.

This therapeutic structure defines the therapy experience as a place where feelings and emotions will be examined and discussed but not acted upon. Occasionally the therapist will ask the family not to discuss certain sensitive issues outside of the therapy session in order to control the potential for impulsive escalation. Often families will respond to these rules with a sense of relief and accept them as a way of containing and managing the uncontrollable emotions they experience at home. We cannot overemphasize the importance of establishing this early structure. In our practices we have seen too many cases in which therapists failed to recognize the intensity and potential for violent escalation in the borderline family with the result that the therapy went destructively out of control. Once this has occurred, the therapist has seriously weakened not only his or her therapeutic control but has also lost the credibility and power to manage and contain the uncontrollable parts of the family's life that they had entrusted to the therapist.

Once the therapeutic structure has been established it must be maintained throughout the course of treatment. One of the most important aspects of maintaining this structure, aside from enforcing the aforementioned rules, is for the therapist to keep his or her part of the bargain. This means keeping appointments as scheduled and, of course, being on time. As we identified previously, many therapists have discussed with us their own personal reactivity to borderline families, which often takes the form of canceling or being chronically late for appointments. In one such case a therapist was delayed by an emergency in his office. After 10 minutes his secretary advised the family that he would be delayed another 5 or 10 minutes. When he went to the reception area 20 minutes late to greet and apologize to the borderline family they arose indignantly, shouted angry comments about his lack of interest in them, and knocked over a lamp as they rushed out of the office. They did not return to therapy.

In a similar manner, the structure is maintained by the therapist's appropriately timed expressions of caring and genuine support coupled with a clear sense of professionalism. The therapist must use the structure to set carefully the range of closeness and distance for each family system. It is often this dimension of clinical intervention that inexperienced therapists will mishandle in working with borderline families. It is particularly important that the therapist not initiate joining the system too soon or encourage intimacy prematurely, which will cause the family to withdraw and perhaps not return to therapy. The borderline family's boundaries must be recognized and respected. This is particularly difficult for the inexperienced or impatient therapist who may have difficulty in "reading" the vulnerabilities and protection level of boundaries in the system, as well as in being able to gently and cautiously move toward and away from the system.

After the therapy process is under way, the maintenance of this structure serves to allow the family to begin gradually to tolerate conflict and distortion without splitting and projection. It also allows the family to experience some controlled verbalized aggression without destructive consequences. Often the role of the therapist becomes that of a "model" of interaction within the family. This modeling may be explicit. For example, the therapist may point out to a family that the mother's fury toward the therapist when she thought he or she had been siding with the "bad" son was not so overwhelming that they could not work things out successfully between them. This modeling experience will help when the parents are struggling with "owning" their own anger and learning to be direct with one another despite their fear of destroying each other.

Jim Singleton is a 43-year-old university professor with a Ph.D. in theater (see Figure 4–4). He was an only child and reported that while his mother "adored" him, she was "forced to leave" him at the age of 8. She moved to another city to care for his sick father from whom she had been separated for several years. Nevertheless, he reported that he continues to be "very close" to his mother. As a child Jim was moved from relative to relative and had to rely on his ability to ingratiate and entertain others to make himself feel accepted. He appears quite charming in therapy and cooperative in his declaration that he would "do anything" to help Billy.

Mary Singleton is 39 and the youngest of three daughters. Her father deserted the family when she was only 5. She described her role in her family of origin as the "supporter and caretaker" of her mother and the "hand-maiden" to her

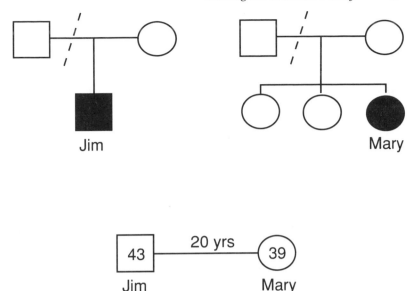

FIGURE 4–4. Jim's and Mary's Families of Origin

"narcissistic" sisters. Mary continues to play the role of caretaker even now in her family of origin. She is called upon frequently to assist in solving problems and disputes in the family even though she lives 500 miles away in another state.

Jim and Mary have been married 20 years. They met shortly after Jim had received his Ph.D. and began his first teaching position in a rural midwestern town. Linda, their first child, was born later in that first year of their marriage. Billy arrived 4 years later, and Cindy was born 2 years after that. When Jim and Mary were first asked about their relationship, both insisted that they had a very happy marriage with few problems. They maintained that the only difficulties they had ever experienced in their family were the result of Billy's disobedience and selfishness. When they were asked to describe how they managed marital conflict, they agreed that Jim withdrew while Mary pursued him until anger erupted. This was followed by a period of emotional distancing.

In general, the therapist will observe that the borderline families in the assessment category of low structural flexibility will more frequently test the strength and limits of the therapeutic structure from the onset of therapy. These families' own rigidly defined structures and internal vulnerabilities make the prospect of accommodating to an external structure, such as therapy, both scary and threatening. These families will often test the therapeutic structure, much as a child "bumps up against" a parent's rules.

Thus the initial careful evolution of a clear therapeutic structure is critical to providing control and safety in the early phases of treatment. As therapy progresses, this structure will provide a gradually acceptable milieu for the containment of impulses and anger.

> *Jim and Mary arrived for the initial family therapy session with Billy and Cindy. Linda, the eldest daughter, was away at college in another state. However, Linda and her mother kept in close contact by phone and wrote letters to one another at least once or twice a week. Linda was described as being somewhat depressed about leaving home for college this year. Mary was also concerned that Linda was eating too much and that she would become overweight.*
>
> *In this initial session (2 hours), the family appeared battle-worn and frightened. Billy displayed a somewhat arrogant style and continually looked out the window. Jim was slumped down in a chair next to Billy, appearing passive and timid. Mary sat rigidly on the edge of the couch attempting to contain her bitter anger, while Cindy was huddled like a frightened rabbit in her mother's lap. As they each began to describe how they viewed the problems within the family, Billy would interrupt with intimidating outbursts. After about 30 minutes, this escalated into a verbal attack directed toward his mother. The therapist intervened and told Billy to stop, stating that this behavior could not be allowed in the therapy sessions. The therapist then explained to the entire family the rule that verbal or physical attacks were not permitted. To Mary's surprise, Billy conformed to the rule. During the remainder of the first hour of the session Billy was cooperative and even somewhat charming toward the therapist. However, his ability to contain his impulsive outbursts deteriorated and he was confronted again by the*

therapist. This time he became verbally abusive toward the therapist. At first this was ignored and attention was directed toward the mother. However, he continued to escalate this and threatened to push over a piece of furniture. Since this could no longer be ignored, the therapist told him that if he continued any of this behavior he would have to leave the office. The tension in the entire room became potentially explosive with the other family members waiting to see what would transpire. Their concerns regarding safety issues within the therapy sessions were real and they obviously wondered if Billy's persecutory behavior would intimidate the therapist.

Billy refused to leave and challenged the therapist to make him leave. He was told that a therapist from another office would be called in to assist in removing him and that he had a choice to make. The mother was then engaged, while Billy was muttering under his breath, and asked if this was what it was like at home. Mary seemed to relax and affirmed that, indeed, it was. Once again it was made clear that physical or emotional attacks would not be tolerated. The family was told that this would be a safe place to deal with the intense emotions that must have felt overwhelming to them. Everyone, including Billy, appeared to relax at this point. They were beginning to feel safe. The process of disengaging from Billy when the tension was high and engaging the mother by way of identification with her was a successful joining maneuver and served to diffuse the escalation. Mary reported that this was the first time that someone outside of the family had really seen and experienced what was going on and what they had lived with. She said she had a sense of relief and hoped that they might be helped.

At the end of this initial session the parents were asked to return without the children. This was done with an element of mystery so that the children and parents would wonder what was happening and whether they were indeed being excluded. Jim and Mary appeared visibly relieved. The fee, times for appointments, and policy regarding cancellations were presented and agreed upon. The parents were asked directly not to discuss events in the session with the children because it would only escalate the conflict, which at this point was unresolvable at home. They were encouraged to talk with one another. Additionally they were told not to punish Billy for his behavior since he had performed his "job" well for the family and the therapist in demonstrating what occurs in the family. They were also told not to respond to any of Billy's further reactions after the session, but Jim was asked to physically intervene and actively support Mary when this negative interactional loop was enacted again at home.

This initial session is often typical of borderline families with a dominant persecuting child. The inclination of either the inexperienced or individually oriented therapist is typically not to subject himself or herself to the chaos of the entire family but to see the child individually or the parents separately. The error in failing to see the entire system is that the critical dimensions of parent-child interactions are lost and the necessary beginning intervention of establishing strong therapeutic structures is bypassed. There is no question that for the family therapist to be effective with borderline families he or she must be able to accommodate to anger and chaos and establish firm therapeutic control.

In this case, the primary struggle was establishing the therapeutic structure in order to ensure the family's safety from Billy's rage and from any expected reprisals from the therapist. Both the therapist and Billy verbalized some anger but it was not acted upon. The initial structure was maintained by joining with the mother in order to demonstrate to both parents alternate ways of disengaging from the cycle of escalation with Billy. The assignments to the parents were attempts to solidify the therapeutic structure and to generalize from what had occurred in the session to management issues for them at home. An implicit sense of hope was implanted that some things could be handled differently with more positive outcomes.

We need to be clear here for family therapists who might be reading strategic/paradoxical messages into the above case process that these interventions and assignments were directed explicitly at structural and management issues and that they had no other strategic or paradoxical intent. We will discuss later our observations that paradoxical interventions intended to unbalance or confuse borderline systems in the early stages of therapy can be dangerous and potentially explosive.

REALITY TESTING WITH THE
FAMILY IN THERAPY

The borderline family's experience and perception of reality tend to be narrow and rigid with characteristic distortions of issues and events both within and without the system. This poor range of reality testing limits severely the availability of external feedback as an informational resource. The system's external boundaries tend to be closed so that the family functions within its own narrowly constructed perception of reality, which may have been transmitted across several generations. These closed boundaries not only reinforce the potential for internal distortions but also pose a difficult task for the therapist in the early phases of engaging and joining the system.

The clinical task of reality testing is employed across a broad range of cases, but it becomes a major component of family therapy with borderline families due to their typically excessive distortions. Thus the therapist must possess the personal skills and resources to represent and model a form of consensually validated external reality and to bring this to bear on the perceptual and affective distortions of the family. *The family therapist's goal is to join and enter the system, experience with the family members their contextual distortions, and gradually challenge inaccurate perceptions and confirm more objective and functional data.*

This process of joining a system therapeutically is critical to a therapist's ability both to assess accurately the dynamics of the system and to gain a level of therapeutic control by which to move the system to new levels of accommodation. The process of actually joining a family system is often difficult for therapists trained in individual psychotherapy. It involves more than the establishment of rapport or a therapeutic alliance. "Joining" defines essentially the therapist's actual movement into the life and process of the system. Readers who are unfamiliar with this clinical process are referred to broader works in family therapy (e.g., Minuchin & Fishman, 1981; Nichols & Everett, 1986) for a further explication of this and other methods of initiating family therapy.

The therapist will recognize distortions within the borderline family, which include at least three interlocking processes: (1) splitting and projective identification; (2) erratic control swings within the parent-child subsystem; and (3) collective despair. The interlocking processes of splitting and projective identification are often subtle, but nevertheless, identifying them will get to the root of major ingrained distortions. As we have described, the parents may split their children into roles of "good" and "bad." A son, such as Billy, may be seen as all bad and a daughter may be viewed as all good regardless of either one's actual behavior. Within the developmental life of a borderline family these projections will distort the children's own perceptions of themselves. As these split perceptions are "accepted" by the respective children they will begin to behave accordingly in ways that will be clearly displayed for the therapist.

Borderline families also display erratic parental control swings within the parent-child subsystem. The therapist will observe these in the often extreme and unpredictable shifts in discipline which may range from abusive control to abandonment to a bitter laissez-faire position. After a period of time, the children's perceptions of their parents' roles and of their own positions within the family will become confused and fragmented. This was illustrated in the Singleton family when Jim would vacillate from ignoring Billy's behavior to physically fighting with him in order to control him. Mary also exhibited this pattern when she became exhausted from keeping "a close eye on him and his whereabouts." When she found that this was not sufficient to control him, she would swing to a more withdrawn position of "giving him enough rope to hang himself."

The therapist will observe that the affect and mood of a borderline family tend to lie within a very limited and narrow range. We have characterized this as *collective despair*. The broader expectable range of emotions that encompasses joy, humor, or hope appears to be foreign to the borderline system. The therapist will often be puzzled when his or her own use of these emotions in the therapy process gains no reciprocal response. This is frustrating and often intimidating to inexperienced therapists who have not gained confidence in utilizing a broad range of affective resources in joining a system.

The role of the therapist in reality testing within the borderline family begins during the early process of joining the system through often casual efforts to confirm and support whatever aspects of the family's perceptions appear more accurate and grounded in reality. In a case in which a mother clung tenaciously to the split perceptions of the children, the therapist observed that the father occasionally acknowledged some good behavior in the "bad" son. By identifying and exploring this, the therapist helped the father to realize that in fact he rarely acknowledged such good behavior when the mother was present. This limited observation became an important early resource by which the therapist cautiously began to challenge the broader distortions within the system.

After these carefully chosen early challenges to some minor distortions have been accomplished, often quite casually, the therapist must then begin to identify and confront more significant distortions as they occur in the therapy process. Since such distortions are intrinsic to the family's everyday interaction, the therapist will be able to observe them readily throughout the family therapy process. For example, when a father is portrayed as ineffective, the therapist might observe that he has always responded well to questions and has indeed raised the children in a competent manner: "Perhaps it is only when you and your wife are involved in parenting activities together that you see yourself in this way. In fact, you probably do a pretty good job with the children on your own."

By offering these types of observations within the context of the family system, the therapist can use the power of his or her role to confirm for the system a new reality for the father. An observation such as this, when stated clearly or even dramatically or humorously, cannot be ignored, and it forces the system to accommodate in some manner. However, these more direct confrontations can be effective only after a firm therapeutic structure is in place.

In a similar manner the therapist must intervene and interrupt interactions to encourage family members to "own" split-off parts of themselves that have been projected onto others. In the preceding example, the therapist would support the father in working through the uncomfortable aspects of "owning" the split-off competency part of himself. The therapist might need to identify intergenerational role models and attachment patterns which reinforced the perception of male parenting incompetency over several generations. At the same time the therapist would push the family to struggle to accept this new information regarding the competency of the father as parent. This latter intervention is in response to the power of the reciprocal and circular interactional patterns within the family. To ignore these and deal simply with the father's internal issues would naively ignore the expectable sabotaging of this role by other family members and the father's eventual abandonment of the new data.

A session from the Singleton case presents several examples of reality testing. This session occurred during the second half of the treatment when Mary began to be less dependent on Jim, able to set limits with him, and no longer "wait on him." During this session, Mary interrupted Jim and would not let him speak for her. Then suddenly she withdrew, returning to her passive/dependent position in their interaction. When questioned by the therapist, she reported experiencing intense guilt and said she felt "very selfish." The therapist affirmed for her that wishing to speak for herself certainly was not selfish, and encouraged her to do more of it. Jim reacted as if he'd been hurt and lamented, "Mary acts like she doesn't want my help any more." When questioned by the therapist on how he was feeling, Jim admitted that he was angry that Mary was becoming more independent but also admitted that in some ways it was a relief from his having to feel "responsible for everything and everybody." The therapist then pointed out to Mary that indeed, she was not hurting Jim by setting limits with him; he was, in some ways freed up and "relieved." The therapist reframed that by setting limits Mary was giving Jim the room to become more emotionally independent himself.

The therapist asked Mary about the intensity of her guilt and feelings of selfishness. She began to cry and told of being so afraid of becoming "self-centered" like her "narcissistic" sisters. The therapist asked Jim his opinion of her fear—how realistic was it? He affirmed with examples from his observations of her family that Mary was, indeed, "not at all like her sisters!" Mary was encouraged by the therapist to "take these data in" and begin to get an internal sense of the difference between feeling a good sense of self and "being selfish." Jim, reciprocally, moved from being Mary's "caretaker" to a more partner-peer position by sharing his perceptions of her family; this reinforced Mary's owning her previously split-off sense of self, that she had labeled and feared as selfish.

With interventions such as these (interrupting interactional sequences, challenging distortions, reframing [see below] and identifying intergenerational roots), the therapist helped the Singletons to reality test old perceptions and own new more accurate perceptions of themselves and others.

Reality testing with the borderline family is also aided by the technique of *reframing*. Here a sensitive issue or dysfunctional behavior may be restated in such a manner that the family can accept it without feeling threatened. This is much like viewing the differing reflections of a multi-faceted diamond—the therapist simply feeds back differing and richer aspects of the family's own reality. For example, a spouse's distancing may be reframed as sensitivity to the other's needs for separateness. The disruptive behavior of the persecuting child may be reframed as an effort by the child to keep the family together. In the Singleton case, the therapist reframed Billy's disruption of the first session as his service to the therapy and the family by showing the therapist how it really was at home. With Jim and Mary, the therapist reframed what felt "selfish" to Mary (setting limits with Jim) as an act of caring, as Jim was relieved of carrying all the responsibility alone.

We have found reframing to be a particularly useful resource with borderline families. At one level it acknowledges the behavioral aspects of a distortion, while at another it plays into the system's protective need to be in control by defining the problem. The therapist then uses these two dimensions of the clinical process to gently add a new aspect to the system's reality. However, the therapist must always be careful that the data or behavior being reframed is congruent with the family's reality. If the content of the reframe is merely a fabrication done to challenge or perturb the system, it will have a negative impact by injecting further distortions into the system and may even provoke a withdrawal or chaotic reaction by the family. Inexperienced therapists may "get away with" ill-conceived reframes in families that are functioning at a higher level, but the consequences with a borderline family could be disastrous.

As we suggested earlier, we want to particularly caution less experienced therapists in the use of strategic or paradoxical techniques with borderline families. We certainly use strategic techniques in our own practices and view them as potentially powerful resources in the hands of skilled family therapists who recognize clearly the technical assessment data of the system. However, we have seen too many borderline cases that were treated by careless strategic interventions which were perceived distrustfully by the family as manipulation and in some cases led to explosive and destructive acting out. We recognize that inexperienced family therapists may gravitate to dramatic interventions observed in weekend workshops. However, effective strategic skills can best be learned under supervision and should not be "tested" randomly on borderline families.

The overall strategies suggested in reality testing with the borderline family are intended to correct the system's perceptual and affective distortions, as well as to perturb the system in a way that causes it to struggle on its own to accommodate new information. Obviously the role of reality testing occurs throughout the therapy process, and certain strategies may be repeated many times.

> *Over the initial 4 to 6 weeks of therapy the issues of discipline and control of Billy remained central. Jim and Mary were usually seen together without the children. The initial goal was to interrupt the intensity of conflict between Mary and Billy by gradually moving Jim into the interactive cycle. During these sessions, all the reality testing interventions described earlier were utilized by the therapist. For example, a focus at this time was on correcting the distorted perceptions of both Jim and Mary. One of Jim's distortions was that he was too gentle and sensitive a man to deal strongly with Billy (he thus disowned the more aggressive part of his nature that would aid him in taking a stronger stand with Billy). One of Mary's distorted perceptions was that she was a harsh mother, trying to keep Billy from getting out of control (thus, disowning her own fear of losing control). The therapist often reframed Jim's gentleness and sensitivity as being his strength in engaging Billy because Jim's approach was more indirect and less emotionally threatening to Billy. Mary's harshness was reframed as her ability to "take a strong stand" and to "take control" by withdrawing from the conflict with Billy when it became clear that it was only escalating. As Mary*

disengaged from Billy and Jim became more involved, the conflict continued but Jim could disengage from the cycle much more readily than Mary. However, even though this intervention began to change patterns within the system, Billy responded by escalating the conflict even more until the parents had to seek legal intervention for fear of physical violence. The court provided a sort of ultimate limit setting, reality testing function with consequences outside the family. A probation officer was assigned who worked with the therapist and the parents to set up realistic rules and consequences for Billy. Jim and Mary began to feel that they finally had some power even though Billy predictably tested the limits. After several incidents he learned that the consequences were going to be consistent. As the parental alliance developed and improved through the first 3 months of therapy, Billy's persecutory behavior ceased, and the parents were even able to report that he was enjoyable around the house, thus reinforcing new perceptions and a new role for Billy in the family.

The establishment of the early therapeutic structure and reality testing interventions directed toward disengaging Mary from the conflictual cycle with Billy and enhancing a clear parental alliance had been successful. The projective identification loop between Mary and Billy had been potent within the system. It appeared that Billy had come to "own" Mary's unfulfilled adolescent rebelliousness and grandiosity, while Mary had "owned" in complementary fashion Billy's fear of dependency and vulnerability. Even an experienced family therapist might be deceived into feeling that the problems presented in this case had been resolved quite successfully. However, this structural re-alignment simply identified the next dysfunctional level of the system. In this case, the improvement in Billy's behavior created an expectable systemic imbalance which allowed the formerly latent stress within the spousal subsystem to appear. Mary reported spending longer periods on the phone with Linda, the "good" child who was now away at college. She even suggested that Linda come home for a weekend visit.

At this point in therapy Mary became somewhat distant and aloof with the therapist. As Jim became more engaged in the therapy and interested in working on marital issues, Mary found excuses to miss several sessions in a row. She was reportedly agitated at home and angry at the therapist. The therapist decided not to challenge directly her absences, believing that Mary would have expected that and possibly withdrawn further. Rather, the therapist decided to play into the system's new imbalance and agreed to see Jim separately. Jim was delighted to have the separate attention. In these sessions he portrayed Mary has having such "low self-esteem" that she could not trust anyone. He had confronted her in the past with her inability to be flexible and to allow him any freedom in the relationship. His portrayal continued with Mary cast as the "sick" one, which she had "proven" by her missed appointments. Here the therapist aligned with Jim's self-assigned role of "co-therapist" and challenged him to help bring Mary back to therapy. He achieved this 2 weeks later. After that conjoint session, Mary was seen individually for three sessions to re-balance the therapy process and thus equalize the relative involvement of both spouses. This also served to remove Jim from the role of "co-therapist" and return him to that of spouse.

The clinical data thus far illustrate how the family therapist must always be "one step ahead" of the system in anticipating potential reciprocal responses following inter-ventions which create structural imbalances. It also il-lustrates well the role of the therapist in joining the life and flow of the system rather than challenging or confronting it too directly. The therapist's decision to play into Mary's resistance and align with Jim was successful. The ex-perienced family therapist is always watching the flow of the system and determining alternative responses. Here an al-ternate strategy might have been to recall the whole family for several sessions as Billy's behavior improved. This might have kept the mother involved via this success and it would have served to delay premature focus on the marriage which is probably what evoked Mary's resistance.

In Mary's individual sessions she revealed that she was afraid that she would be labeled "crazy," which is how her husband and two prior therapists had seen her. She explained that she did not see herself as so "pathologically dependent

*and rigid" as they had portrayed her in the prior therapy ex-
perience. She felt capable of flexibility and independence, but
when confronted by Jim she would become confused and begin
to believe that he was right. She also suggested that Jim was
really the dependent one despite his apparent self-reliance,
though when she had mentioned this to him he had become
furious and withdrawn. Several more concurrent individual
sessions for both Jim and Mary were useful in strengthening a
therapeutic alliance with both. For Mary this served to modu-
late her fear of closeness and apprehension about the
therapist. Jim used these sessions to test the trust level for
revealing some of his own vulnerabilities.*

A potential danger in seeing spouses concurrently in individual sessions for very long is that one or the other will attempt to triangle the therapist into a coalition around
spousal relationship issues. This occurred here as Jim
talked in admiring terms and at length about the therapist (a
female) to Mary. He seemed to do this to arouse jealousy but
he had always denied any "physical affair." Mary later confronted the therapist with this with a real edge of anger. If
the therapist had not been successful in establishing an effective therapeutic structure to deal with this, Mary could
have launched into the therapist in an effort to make her the
bad object to replace Billy's role.

INTERACTIONAL DISENGAGEMENT

As we have discussed, the highly enmeshing process of
the borderline family requires the therapist to devise interventions intended to disengage members from their interactional intensity and projective identification. The latter
phenomenon is particularly difficult to challenge in the borderline family because the members function as if they are
joined symbiotically in their reciprocally distorted perceptual
and behavioral patterns. In addition, the system over time
has functioned to set these interactional patterns rigidly into
its structure and process. Thus, as with reality testing, the
process of interactional disengagement must be expected to
occur and be repeated throughout the course of therapy. The
clinical task here is to create and "mark" boundaries around

individual members of the system and the three major sub-systems. This process restores an appropriate level of ambivalence to the interactions of the system so that members begin to relate as whole persons with both good and bad elements.

A major strategy in the process of interactional disengagement is the identification, often graphically, of the projective identification loop. We have found this to be most effective when video or audio tapes can be played back for the family. Here the therapist might point out specific intervals when one member "invites" and the other "accepts" projected issues, or when typical escalation and outcome patterns can be observed. This technique appears to objectify these processes for the family and allow them to gain some distance from it. Gradually members can identify their emotions which are evoked in the process and recognize how they feel "hooked" and "victimized" by the sequence. This serves to diffuse and de-intensify the reactive aspects of the projective loop and make them seem more manageable.

When the therapist is working in a co-therapy team, additional strategies become available. For example, one therapist may remain "outside" of the system to provide stability and objectivity while the other therapist "enters' the system in an effort to pull one selected member out of the projective loop and into an alliance with the therapist. This could be accomplished much in the manner in which Zuk (1981) utilized "side-taking" and Bowen (1978) "detriangling." Such an intervention interrupts the projective loop by temporarily disengaging one member from the interactive intensity. This allows some new information and reality to be fed in and at the same time requires the system to begin to accommodate to this enforced imbalance.

Another interaction disengagement strategy involves utilizing the power of silence to interrupt the projective loop and cut off the escalation. For example, if the object of the identified projection is instructed by the therapist not to respond, to leave the room, or to change the subject under certain circumstances, the projecting member has no "container" in which to "dump" the projection and must begin to own the issues for himself or herself. The therapist should anticipate that such an intervention is more difficult than it sounds because there is often a subtle rule operating within borderline families that "the one who has the last word has the power."

> *Interactional disengagement tactics were utilized early with the Singleton family by identifying the interactional loop with Billy. Here Billy would bait Mary with an ostensibly reasonable request such as using the car to take something to a friend's house 3 miles away. Mary would agree but tell him to return directly home. Billy would counter that he needed to stop at the store and Mary would say no. Billy would become insulting; Mary would respond similarly and accuse him of always behaving this way. As this escalated Mary would insist that he get out of the car, Billy would refuse, and a screaming stand-off would ensue. These interactional situations would occur repeatedly over a variety of issues. They would end with Mary furious but guilty, wondering if she had been too harsh, thus "owning" Billy's own harshness and disrespect. Here the therapist encouraged the triangulation of the father into the interactional scene to serve to diffuse the intensity between Mary and Billy and to allow Mary to disengage. The therapist also encouraged Mary to "be silent" and even to walk away from Billy to disengage herself from the intensity. Mary noticed that when she did remove herself or refused to argue, she felt less harsh and more reasonable, a sign that she was no longer "owning" Billy's harshness. At times she could even empathize with his vulnerability, especially when she was not being harsh.*

Similar projective loops were identified between Jim and Mary. Basically Jim would be overtly supportive of Mary's struggles with esteem while covertly devaluing her, which was indicative of his own low self-esteem. Mary would "own" his projections, feel worse about herself, doubt her own judgment, and behave in a more overtly dependent manner. Thus Mary "owned" and "carried" Jim's low self-esteem, which he found intolerable, while reciprocally Jim "owned" and "carried" aspects of Mary's narcissism, which she found intolerable. These patterns could only have been identified through the *in vivo* data from the ongoing therapy process with the family and couple together.

> *Jim would often begin a therapy session by observing that Mary seemed "down" or depressed, and he would ask the*

therapist to help her. Mary would respond that she was not "particularly" depressed and did not know what Jim was talking about. Jim would then describe her depressive behaviors in such a manner that allowed him to appear both healthy and a psychological expert. The therapist playfully challenged Jim on this expert role and suggested that he liked the limelight too much to give it up. Jim laughed, recalling his professional role in drama. The therapist pushed further, reflectively asking if any situations might have occurred recently that caused Jim to feel depressed. He looked shocked and replied that he had been turned down for a promotion at the university several weeks ago and that he had not shared this with Mary. He began immediately to avoid further discussion of this or of the feelings potentially associated with it.

The process of disengaging Jim and Mary from these interactive patterns was difficult. Jim had to experience these feelings of inferiority and emptiness in order to recognize how his need to feel "good" was used to cover them up. Gradually he could identify his reactive feelings toward the dependency and low self-esteem that Mary portrayed. He also understood that "owning" the narcissistic pieces of Mary allowed her not to be threatened by her own grandiose and greedy feelings. Mary gradually recognized how her self-effacing style effectively covered these feelings. In therapy each was encouraged to explore these aspects of themselves in the context of intergenerational patterns observed and learned in their families of origin. Often looking at patterns across generations feels safer to spouses than confronting the sensitive aspects of those same issues between one another. All of these resources were implemented over a 6-month period with the focus primarily on Jim and Mary, and these changes enhanced the ongoing interactional disengagement process within the rest of the system.

WORKING WITH THE INTERGENERATIONAL SYSTEM

We have identified previously the intergenerational patterns of the borderline family, which are characterized by enmeshing loyalties and rigid structures which dysfunctionally bind one generation to the next. The inexperienced family therapist should not view intergenerational work as merely the collection of genogram and traditional social history data. Instead it should be viewed as the weaving of a dramatic scenario by a master storyteller with the actual players and remnants of the system's rich history present in the office.

When intergenerational issues or loyalties actively intrude into the present functioning of the family, the therapist may need to focus explicitly on these issues. However, as is more generally the case in family therapy, the therapist moves in and out of these intergenerational issues according to the flow and process of the therapy. Often, passing comments by a family member can lead to important observations regarding comparative interactional patterns and historical reflections. The value of working with family of origin data occurs first at the level of objectifying and clarifying historical issues and patterns, and second at the level of disengaging family members from repetitious historical and emotionally binding patterns.

For example, a wife may reflect on her "helpless" role in the family and her reactivity to degrading remarks from her persecuting son. With the emotional reactivity as a clue to existing intergenerational issues, the therapist may ask her to examine patterns that she may have experienced growing up in her own family. She may recall how angry and powerless she felt as a child when persistently devalued by her father. A strategic move of actually "placing blame" within a family of origin pattern actually serves both to diffuse immediate experiences and to begin to objectify the issues. The extent to which "blame" is left in the family of origin will vary according to member's ability to "own" these patterns. The therapist's task is to prompt and pursue affective exchanges around these patterns within the spousal or nuclear system. Intergenerational distortions and loyalties must be experienced by family members at a new level, and not simply as cognitive exercises, in order to broaden boundaries and diffuse repetitious interactional loops.

The next step in intergenerational work is to decide whether or not it would be useful clinically to invite family of origin members to the therapy sessions. Often this takes considerable preparation time for family members due to their fear of and anticipated vulnerability to having their parent actually in the therapy room with them (see Williamson, 1981, 1982 a,b). Inexperienced therapists should be cautious here, because even the suggestion of this intervention may trigger unexpected reactivity and cause a family to withdraw from therapy. When the therapist believes that active family of origin intrusions and loyalties are so great or would significantly facilitate therapy, movement toward inviting selected family of origin members should proceed.

The therapist must recall that in borderline families certain family of origin members may be the object or source of primitive idealizations and projections. These often latent or hidden dimensions typically will trigger intense fear and apprehension, which will be shared by the entire system. If the inexperienced therapist is still not sure how to recognize a system's protective closing of external boundaries to a therapist, this suggestion will usually provoke such a response.

Family of origin members may be invited to join the ongoing therapy on a regular basis or to attend periodically as "consultants." The latter strategy is more common with borderline families and produces less threat to all parties. Often just the preparations for inviting a family of origin member will evoke such intense feelings that there will be major therapeutic movement even before the event occurs. Typically the response is to pull formerly discordant family members together in a uniquely supportive and collusive manner to protect a member, and thus the system, from a fear of being overwhelmed by a parent.

These interventions can be dramatic for the borderline family, but it is our recommendation that the inexperienced therapist attempt such a strategy only when on-site supervision is available from a seasoned family therapist. The potential for loss of therapeutic control and destructive behavior is great. However, such interventions can dramatically challenge distortions and long-standing coalitions as well as diffuse historical and present splitting and projective patterns. As the power of these distortions subsides there will be a diminution of both family of origin loyalties and repetitive interactional patterns. This allows greater personal availability of members to the nuclear system as well as increased bonding and trust with the therapist.

Mary's parents and sisters lived some distance away, so when the therapist learned that she would be visiting in her hometown for several days, the opportunities to bring more "live" intergenerational data into therapy was apparent. In reviewing her visit home, she identified the fear that she would appear again to be just like her self-centered sisters. She also identifed considerable continuing anger at her mother for not being powerful enough to stop the sisters from making servants out of both her and her mother. In the therapy session before leaving on her trip, the therapist "coached" (see Bowen, 1978) her to keep a little distance from her sisters and re-experience the emotional pull back into that familiar but uncomfortable pattern. Upon her return she expressed some guilt because she did not successfully keep her distance from the sisters. However, upon reflection she had objectified the events sufficiently to recognize some of her own emotional needs which her mother never met, and that in fact she did not behave like her sisters and no longer needed to fear that she would become like them.

Jim's work in therapy had focused for a while on the "actor's" role in his family and how this had taken the place of the support and love he sought and still needed. He was particularly infatuated with how this had perhaps led him into the choice of a teaching career in the theater. The therapist continued to dramatize the acting metaphor for Jim, even to the point of connecting it to his recent failure to gain a promotion. The intent here was to play into this interest and focus on a "safer" issue than his own personal emptiness in the marriage. Even though he described his relationship with his mother as "very close," it was in fact distant with only irregular visits. The therapist suggested to Jim that he play the role of producer/director in orchestrating an invitation for his mother to come for a visit to learn more about his teaching activities and to "consult" in therapy. Jim agreed fairly readily, though he almost backed out the week of the visit. The actual therapy session with the mother present was dramatic and poignant. After very little was said, Jim began crying openly, feeling the loss and emptiness that had haunted him for most of his life. Fortunately both his mother and Mary were responsive (the children were not present for this session), and Jim made an important step toward allowing his emotions to emerge.

The therapist should never underestimate the potential power for borderline families in processing intergenerational loyalties and issues. As we have seen, Jim and Mary opened up new personal directions in a fairly dramatic experiential manner that may have taken months or years in a more cognitively based style of individual psychotherapy. In addition, working these issues out in the presence of one another served to clarify distortions and gradually enhance the marital alliance.

SOLIDIFICATION OF THE MARITAL ALLIANCE AND SIBLING SUBSYSTEMS

As the work of family therapy progresses to diffuse the interactional distortions, both internally and intergenerationally for the family, it is possible to begin to mark and set new internal boundaries and renegotiate more clearly defined alliances within the parent-child subsystem. In treating borderline families, the therapist will often move back and forth between marital and parenting issues, depending on the particular patterns and sensitivities within the system.

The therapeutic task of solidifying the marital alliance involves strengthening the boundaries of the spousal subsystem, reducing intergenerational loyalties of both spouses, and detriangling the "good" and "bad" children, which will remove them from the spousal subsystem triangles and return them to appropriate sibling subsystem roles. These clinical issues are interwoven circularly within the nuclear system, and therapeutic progress is dependent on a balanced movement in all directions. The inexperienced therapist might find it much easier to focus, for example, on the marital alliance. But unless some progress has been made in containing the persecuting behavior of the "bad" child the parents will not be able to disengage from the parent-child dilemmas.

Similarly, the role of the omnipotent child represents an intrusion into the boundaries of the spousal subsystem. The more active and powerful this pseudo-parentified child is, the less privacy and bonding can be expected between the spouses. While the focus in treating borderline families is frequently on the disruptive behavior of the persecuting child, as was the case with the Singleton family, the omnipotent child is often more difficult to deal with because of his or her subtle and insidious power in the system. In fact the inexperienced therapist will often overlook the projective process idealizing this child. Therapeutically the clinician cannot focus directly on this child because he or she is protected by the idealization and the parents will tenaciously cling to this child's "good" role as proof that they are not bad parents. While this child never has the overt power of the parentified child in other family systems, the parents will nevertheless fall back on him or her for support. This child is also used through comparison to further dramatize the "badness" of the persecuting child.

It has been our observation that if the therapist gets "seduced" into trying to pull either of these children out of their assigned roles prematurely the potential imbalance will cause either the boundaries to constrict, closing out the therapist, or the borderline carrier to begin acting out in more regressive and perhaps suicidal ways. The reader may wonder why we have not focused more on the often bizarre and disruptive behaviors typically demonstrated by the borderline carrier that are familiar to all therapists. We are not suggesting that they do not occur in family therapy. However, to the extent that the therapist can construct a successful therapeutic structure and maintain it while at the same time engaging the system and working to keep the various roles and dynamics in some balance, the more likely it is that this individual symptomatology will remain contained. This is precisely why we have introduced the term "borderline carrier"—to help the reader understand that focusing on this identified member's symptoms is not always necessary or even therapeutically desirable. This term should convey that while this member carries certain identifiable developmental deficits, he or she represents but one aspect of the complex intergenerational and nuclear constellation of interactive human elements.

As mentioned, the goals of solidifying the marital alliance are dependent not only on containing the persecuting child but also on removing the omnipotent child from the spousal subsystem and returning him or her to the sibling subsystem. The therapist will observe with regard to the balance within the system that as the projective loops with the "bad" child are contained the need within the system for the split and projected role of the omnipotent child diminishes too. Removing the "good" child from within the spousal subsystem is the last necessary step in forming or renewing a clear marital alliance. Thus it carries with it the threat of further exposing vulnerabilities between the spouses in their marital roles.

The other portion of this intervention requires that the omnipotent child be returned successfully to the sibling subsystem. This is often difficult because of the excessive positive attention and reinforcement this child has received from the parents, which will have engendered both resentment and heightened sibling rivalry. This child's position is like that of the corrupt police officer who is sent to prison and put in the midst of the criminals that he or she helped to put there. In fact we have observed that it is often easier to return the persecuting child to a normative role within the sibling subsystem than to accomplish this with the omnipotent child. This is true particularly if there are other siblings who have not been assigned either of these two projected roles. The siblings seem to be able to accept with some relief the changed behavior of the formerly persecuting child, while resentment often lingers toward the omnipotent child. This difficulty is also enhanced because this omnipotent child is more reluctant to give up the attention and power inherent in the pseudo-parentified role.

> *The Singleton family was in ongoing treatment for fourteen months with a three month termination phase. Following the struggle to contain Billy's behavior and return him to the sibling subsystem, steady progress was made around personal, interactional, and intergenerational issues which had inhibited further development of the marital relationship. As the therapy progressed through the six month mark the therapist became more trusted and thus freer to move in directions that more clearly challenged the patterns of the system. Often the movement was in very small increments, frequently in patterns of one step forward and two steps backward. However, during the final stages of therapy it was clear that Jim and Mary could look at themselves and confront one another with an affiliative and often tender quality that had replaced the former demeaning, blaming, and overly enmesh-*

ing patterns that had been prominent. It was at this time in the therapy that Linda, the "good," omnipotent child, made her last effort to remain a part of the marital subsystem. She returned home from college for the summer overweight and "depressed." She attempted to become enmeshed again with her mother by enlisting her help in losing weight and in finding a job. At first Mary responded as she had in the past by becoming overly involved with Linda to the exclusion of Jim. However, both she and Jim saw the danger to their new-found intimacy and brought Linda to a therapy session. The therapist emphasized that Linda could "take good care of herself" by finding her own job and finding support from her peer group. Linda was also encouraged to go to Weight Watchers without her mother so that she could make friends there. Both Mary and Jim agreed to support these autonomous strivings of Linda to network with others her own age outside of the family. In a rather short period of time (several weeks), Linda was able to find a job and began focusing her attention outside the family. By now all of the children took on more age-appropriate roles. The family now seemed to enjoy being together with a feeling of fun beginning to replace the atmosphere of severity and intensity. The therapist had escaped successfully the early seductive trap of the enmeshing system which pulled her into an increasingly confrontive and competitive role with Billy. Utilizing the external influence of the court, the system was stabilized and then moved carefully beyond its former limits to experience new patterns of living together.

Chapter 5

When Hospitalization Is Necessary: Balancing the Roles of Community Therapy and Institutional Treatment

This chapter will explore hospitalization as an integral aspect of family therapy with borderline families. Because of the typical levels of intensity, chaos, and often explosiveness which exist in borderline families, the potential for severe emotional disturbances, acting-out, life-threatening behaviors, or violence is ever-present in borderline families, particularly in the early phases of treatment.

It has been our experience that effective family therapy will reduce dramatically the need for hospitalization by containing and reshaping the dynamics which may trigger such behavior. However, a variety of other variables may influence the potential need for the temporary removal of a family member, whether an identified borderline carrier, a terrorizing "bad" child, or a depressive "good" child, in order to ensure the survival of either that member or the family system itself.

Thus it is important for the therapist who practices independently in the community to arrange effective medical and psychiatric back-up. Typically the levels of intensity or

107

disturbance present when the family is referred for therapy may suggest the need for hospitalization. This potential expectation for hospitalization of a family member may be reinforced by prior treatment experiences in which hospitalization may have been ordered by former therapists for perhaps even minimal disturbances. Of course, other variables involving the skills and experience of the therapist with each particular family system and presenting issues will be influential in the final judgment to hospitalize.

The members of the borderline family system most typically identified for hospitalization are the borderline carrier (in our clinical population most often the mother in the nuclear system) and the persecuting or "bad" child. While the clinician may observe varying levels of depression in the omnipotent or "good" child, the other spouse, or both, these conditions rarely are severe enough to warrant hospitalization.

Since we view hospitalization as an occasionally necessary therapeutic intervention to manage a highly dysfunctional system at a point of disequilibrium, we will address this chapter to the community therapist who is engaged in the treatment of borderline families. It is this therapist who must rely on his or her clinical assessment skills to determine when hospitalization is necessary, and it is this therapist who must work with the institutional treatment team. Thus we will discuss further clinical indicators and precipitants for hospitalization, the impact of hospitalization as a crisis for both the family system *and the family therapy process*, and issues of developing a constructive relationship among hospital, family, and therapists.

PRECIPITATING EVENTS TO HOSPITALIZATION

Jane Walker, a 36-year-old mother of two adolescent children, had been in therapy with individual psychotherapists off and on over the prior 8 years (see Figure 5–1). Shortly after her youngest child, Sarah (named after Jane's mother), had begun kindergarten Jane began to experience periods of severe depression typically involving suicidal gestures. These intensified when her husband, Bill, a 38-year-old physician, decided to leave his medical practice and return to school in

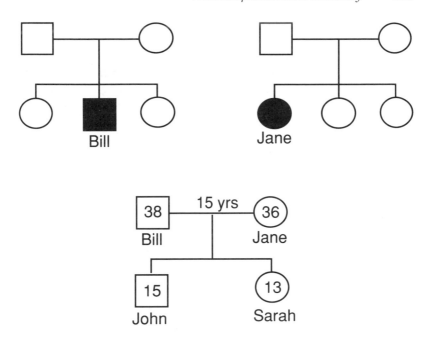

FIGURE 5–1. The Walker Family Genogram

the same community for a specialized residency. Bill was a hard-working physician who had become increasingly unavailable to his wife and children. His decision to return to school represented a certain ambivalence regarding his own success. His father was also a physician in whose medical group Bill practiced. Bill remained more emotionally involved with his family of origin than with his nuclear family.

Jane's prior suicidal gestures had never been life threatening and she had always resisted hospitalization because she felt the children could not manage without her. Jane had begun nursing school but dropped out after her marriage to Bill and subsequent pregnancy. She had played a significant caretaker's role in her family of origin. Her mother had been hospitalized for depression throughout Jane's childhood, and it had been up to Jane, the eldest, to manage her younger sisters, father, and household. Jane's pregnancy with their first child, John, was difficult medically and was punctuated by a serious suicide attempt by her mother 3 weeks before the delivery date. Due to her pregnancy she was unable to rush to her mother's and family's side as she would have done in the past.

Over the ensuing years, as Bill completed medical education and began to practice, the family stabilized somewhat. Jane became quite involved with the young children. John remained something of a problem child, often seen as stubborn and uncooperative. Sarah, their second child, was idealized and went everywhere with her mother. Jane seemed to have been able to balance successfully the emotional involvement with the children and expectations and loyalties with her family of origin until Sarah began school.

Jane's prior therapy had been individually oriented with one therapist making a few feeble attempts to engage Bill. However, Jane's present therapist, who had some limited exposure to family therapy, decided to refer her to a colleague family therapist since the present treatment had served only occasional supportive needs and had not contained the suicidal threats.

Bill was skeptical of any form of expressive therapy and resisted participation for several weeks. The family therapist had refused to begin with Jane until Bill agreed to come to the initial appointment. Bill was adamant about not involving the children in the initial sessions. He could not understand why he should be included in the therapy sessions and attempted unsuccessfully to collude with the referring therapist to take Jane back into individual therapy.

It was perhaps an early error by the family therapist not to insist on the inclusion of the children in the initial sessions. Bill used the time to "dump" his anger and frustration onto Jane, who he perceived as either incompetent as a mother or simply not trying hard enough. At one point she yelled, "Stop treating me like one of your patients!" He retorted, "Stop acting like one," and walked out of the session.

Unfortunately the family therapist had little time to develop any therapeutic structure before precipitating crises began to emerge. It is possible that the earlier inclusion of the children would have diffused some of these interactive issues and allowed some initial emotional containment. Nevertheless, 2 weeks after the initial session, Bill announced that when his residency was completed in 3 months he would be leaving the community to accept an offer in another state. This of course raised dramatic separation issues for both families of origin. The following week Jane's mother took a serious overdose and was hospitalized. Jane became increasingly withdrawn and unavailable, talking continuously of "doing something" to join her mother in the hospital. In consultation with her prior individual therapist, who knew Jane better, it was decided that hospitalization would provide both protection for Jane and some focus and thus containment for the intergenerational turmoil.

Psychiatric hospitalization can be viewed as an auxiliary holding environment that can provide containment when the intensity of rage, depression, or panic reaches such an acute stage that the survival of a member or the system itself is threatened. Often the projective dynamics within the borderline system are directed toward one family member who may respond in a destructive, acting-out manner. The borderline family itself can become caught, inextricably, in an escalating interactive spiral, with dissension and regression between therapy sessions. This leads to a depletion of energy and an inability to perform normative caretaking and nurturant roles within the family and to fulfill work and social responsiblities outside the family.

This situation may reach unmanageable proportions experienced as chaos by both the family and the therapist. Such a pattern is notable in the borderline system with high structural flexibility. The family's desperate need for relief is often expressed in invasive dependency on the therapist, which may be manifested by frequent telephone calls, requests for emergency sessions, and impulsive involvement of community agencies, neighbors, and extended family members. Although this may not lead to hospitalization immediately, if the stress on the family continues unabated, later hospitalization of a family member is often necessary.

In the more isolating borderline systems characterized by low structural flexibility, the emotional escalation creates a more constricted and internally preoccupied response by the system. Typically the internal stress is denied and the family withdraws from potentially supportive resources, including the therapist. Members of the system may cancel appointments, expressing fear that family therapy sessions are exacerbating dangerous emotions. Fantasies of fleeing from the therapy are fueled by projections of distrust and even incompetence onto the therapist. Of course, a thread of reality may trigger these projections when the therapist has not responded to the mounting internal stress and has failed to offer structural containment for the family. Thus the therapist, once viewed as "perfect" and effective, may now become the target of covert devaluation or open hostility.

Both family typologies may eventually reach this phase of chaos and negative projection onto the therapist, requiring hospitalization of a family member. However, this process appears to surface earlier in the family system with low structural flexibility, since this type of family utilizes fewer external resources and functions to further close external boundaries at the earliest escalation of internal stress. Even the most seasoned therapist is susceptible to owning these projected devaluations and experiencing feelings of defeat, followed by a desire to temporarily terminate therapy with the family or simply to give up on treatment.

At this point the therapist not only may feel intimidated by the family dynamics but may also experience a genuine attack on his or her self-esteem. The borderline family may permit the therapist to glimpse what appear to be life and death issues and then quickly hide them away. These experiences often promote in the therapist an insidious oscillating pattern of involvement with the borderline family which can range from hypervigilance to withdrawal. It is often at this juncture that the therapist begins to doubt the accuracy of the assessment and consults with colleagues or supervisors, or seeks a co-therapist.

A complicating factor is the community therapist's own view of hospitalization. Two decades ago most therapists-in-training, regardless of their disciplines, had some exposure to inpatient medical or psychiatric treatment facilities. More recently, the majority of non-medically trained clinicians may never have been in a psychiatric institution or an inpatient psychiatric unit of a medical center. These factors, along with the general movement in the mental health field away from the traditional "medical model" of treatment, have created an interesting disparity between the orientations of community and inpatient therapists. Community therapists have at best an uneasiness with if not a lack of understanding of inpatient treatment resources. Many feel that they are powerful enough to control most dysfunctional behaviors and thus that hospitalization is unnecessary. They often wait until life-threatening behavior becomes apparent. Others feel that the need to utilize hospitalization represents their own impotence and failure as a therapist.

The community therapist who cannot appraise realistically clinical boundaries and limits or who cannot assess accurately the family system's resources, or lack thereof, for managing escalating intensity or certain dysfunctional situations runs the risk of becoming trapped in one of several patterns. The therapist may either intentionally or inadvertently keep the emotional and affective level of the therapy process on such a restricted level that only minimal supportive gestures are made, allowing little or no organizational change. On the other hand, the therapist and family treatment process may become characterized by continual chaos and crisis, which allows very little continuity or stabilization on which change can be based.

These patterns may result in a therapeutic impasse that creates for the therapist and family alike a sense of impotence. It is often at this point that the family may discontinue treatment or that internal dynamics within the system may begin to trigger impulsive or potentially destructive behaviors that will soon be acted out. This is the time when the therapist may be surprised by unanticipated dramatic behaviors which may require hospitalization.

Of course, to avoid such a scenario, the community therapist must learn to recognize and understand the stressors that may push borderline families to a point where some form of hospitalization may be necessary. It is perhaps unfortunate that more settings do not exist in which the entire family system could be "hospitalized," not only to provide containment but also to utilize an institutional structure for systemic reorganization. When such resources are not available, the next best choice involves the temporary removal of one member of the family in order to provide stability and often safety to the entire system as well as to that member. As we have indicated, the member most typically requiring removal is the borderline carrier or the persecuting/bad child.

For the community therapist, there are a variety of internal and situational stressors that serve as indicators for the need for hospitalization (Table 5–1). The therapist can

Table 5–1
POTENTIAL PRECIPITANTS FOR HOSPITALIZATION
OF A MEMBER OF A BORDERLINE FAMILY

Internal System Stressors
  Death of a family of origin parent or other intergenerational
    family member
  Birth of a child
  Illness or loss of a child
  Adolescent's leaving home
  Spouse's return to work or school
  Entrance of an extended family member into the household

External or Situational Stressors
  Geographical relocation from family of origin
  Job loss or significant change
  Serious physical illness
  Injury or disability
  Spouse's return to work or school

anticipate that any unexpected and sudden loss of a family member anywhere throughout the three- or four-generational system will evoke the system's fear of and inability to manage separation. This is particularly true with the death of a close family member. However, the therapist must be aware that in highly enmeshing systems, as we have characterized the borderline system, the death of a family member two or three generations removed from the nuclear system can trigger repercussions intergenerationally. Even unexpected separations or divorces or geographical moves away from the system can trigger a separation crisis. It is the issue of sudden loss that triggers a systemic imbalance which can create waves of panic throughout what is already a tenuously balanced system.

A variety of other factors may have an idiosyncratic impact on certain borderline systems. These may include an adolescent leaving home for the first time, a job loss, marital infidelity, serious physical illness, injury or disability, a spouse going back to school or working outside of the home for the first time, the inclusion of an extended family member into the household, or the birth of a child. It is of course the unexpected events that will trigger the immediate crisis reaction, but even in situations in which such changes are anticipated and planned for, the actual event provoking the threat of separation and loss may still call forth desperate responses. As the community therapist learns to conceptualize the borderline family as a multi-generational system, other potential precipitants will become apparent. From this intergenerational perspective it can be recognized that the closer the events and stressors are to the nuclear borderline system the higher the level of potential reactivity.

In addition to these internal and external precipitating factors, the community therapist must be aware that the treatment process itself may increase the system's internal intensity and thus its crisis potential. There is considerable evidence that in the early stages of family therapy with borderline systems the struggle for structure and control can produce a greater frequency of impulsive and reactive behavior than occurs later in therapy. This may take the form of threatening or suicidal behavior or dramatic acting-out behaviors directed outside the system or back toward members of the system.

As effective family therapy progresses, there are typically fewer reactive behaviors within the system because the therapeutic structure has provided temporary balance and safety for the borderline family. However, in these latter stages of therapy more primitive internal dynamics of individual members and stereotypical interactive patterns and alignments are examined which heightens the emotional intensity both within the borderline system and within the therapist-family treatment system. It is, of course, movement in these areas that begins to push the system beyond a simple homeostatic balance and toward more substantive reorganization and second order change.

Thus, due to the volatility and tenuous balance of the borderline system, the therapist must always monitor potential exacerbating effects of the therapy on the system as possible precipitating events for hospitalization. Even unexpected changes in the role or availability of the therapist can be a trigger. For example, shifting the focus of therapy from a child or parent-child issue to the marital relationship or initiating family of origin work can produce reactive behaviors. A therapist's temporary absence due to illness, vacation, or professional meetings may trigger intense separation reactivity or the perception of rejection on the part of the family.

When one of the authors planned to take an extended 6-week vacation, special arrangements were made for colleagues to provide back-up for three borderline families that had been in therapy for nearly a year. It was interesting that during the 6-week absence, the three cases remained stable with only one telephone call. However, 1 week after the therapist's return to practice, two of the three families began extensive acting-out behavior with a suicide attempt and resultant hospitalization of one member in one family and threatened internal violence and a runaway child in the other family. Our interpretation of this sequence was that the families had pulled together internally to defend against and withstand the stress of the therapist's separation, thus providing a temporary homeostatic binding within the system. This internal regrouping gradually evolved into greater internal stress which was somehow contained by the system until the therapist's return. The renewal of therapy provided the familiarity and safety of the therapeutic structure, which allowed the internal stress to be released in explosive proportions. It was as if therapy then gave the system permission to release the turmoil that it had contained during the therapist's absence. We also speculated on the possibility of displacement from the perceived rejection by the therapist to internal family members or issues.

THE IMPACT OF HOSPITALIZATION ON THE THERAPEUTIC PROCESS AND THE FAMILY SYSTEM

Bill Walker at first opposed the hospitalization, stating that it would become a personal and professional embarrassment. He conceded reluctantly but indicated that he could afford to support the hospitalization for no longer than 6 weeks. Shortly after Jane was admitted, Bill pulled away and would not visit her in the hospital even at the request of her treatment team. Bill also refused to continue with the family therapist.

The children were moved into Bill's parents' home. John soon became increasingly belligerent toward Sarah and even toward his grandmother. Sarah became increasingly withdrawn. Jane's mother was released from the hospital the day after Jane had been admitted. Soon Jane's mother and father began to put pressure on both Jane and Bill to have Sarah, but not John, come to live with them. As a result, Sarah was allowed long periods with Jane's parents, up to 3 or 4 days at a time. This served to heighten the threatening behavior displayed by John and further fragment the family system.

The utilization of psychiatric hospitalization for a member of a borderline family precipitates a trauma of its own for the system and the therapy process. It of course may also exacerbate the presenting dysfunctional behaviors. For the family, hospitalization may represent a sense of failure to contain and manage their own emotions and behaviors. It may also signal a lack of confidence in or sense of failure in the therapy process. As we indicated, it typically causes frustration and a feeling of failure for the community therapist. Of course, the value of hospitalization is that it offers containment and stability during a period of crisis and turmoil, and the vulnerability of the member and system may allow greater access to underlying dynamics and thus greater potential for therapeutic change.

The community therapist who is working with a borderline family in which one member requires hospitalization faces a complex array of variables in the hospital system itself. It is our observation that the therapist's ability to work with the hospital and its therapists, and the hospital's respect for the role of the community therapist and commitment to the value and integrity of the family unit, are central to the therapeutic outcome.

The community therapist, in working with a borderline family at the point of hospitalization, must be able to define an ongoing therapeutic role with the family system itself and evolve a consulting relationship with the inpatient therapists responsible for the hospitalized member. This is not a time for the community therapist to respond to feelings of failure and withdraw from the case. The experienced family therapist will be able to conceptualize the removal of a family member in the broader context of interfacing systems (i.e., outpatient therapy and hospital treatment) and continuing family and intergenerational dynamics.

Systemically, it must be expected that the borderline system as a whole will have to respond in some manner to the absence of a member and rebalance itself. For the less experienced therapist, the drama of hospitalization may become so seductive that the entire focus of ongoing therapeutic responsibility to the family becomes directed toward the hospitalized member. For the experienced family therapist, the absence of a family member is managed in the context of ongoing systemic therapy.

The hospitalization experience may effect borderline systems in several ways. Among the more rigid systems that we have characterized as having low structural flexibility, the removal of a family member by hospitalization will be experienced as an extremely threatening loss. These families will devise numerous diversions and behaviors in an attempt to reunite with the separated member. These may involve excessive phone calls, requests for extra or special visitation privileges, or manipulative efforts to pressure the hospital staff into releasing the member even before stabilization has occurred.

The family system experiences confusion and must deal with the seemingly contradictory dynamics on the one hand of expelling the identified member with the fantasy of forever removing the internal threat, and on the other hand of an intense need to cling to the absent member who serves as a necessary fulcrum for the system's tenuous balance. The resulting ambivalence shared by all family members is often deceptive and confusing to both community and inpatient therapists.

With this family type, the admission process may be aborted several times, only to be reinstituted as the crisis escalates. Family members may offer desperate bargains and bribes in an effort to quickly obtain the return of the absent member. Outspoken family members may make impossible demands or insulting allegations regarding the hospital and its staff as an excuse to withdraw the family member. The hospitalized member and the remainder of the family may vacillate between accepting or rejecting therapy. Here the community therapist can serve a vital role in stabilizing the entire system by continuing the ongoing therapeutic relationship with the remainder of the family system, consulting with inpatient therapists, and often educating the family regarding the goals, structure, and milieu of the hospital setting.

The borderline family typology of high structural flexibility is less rigid and tenuously balanced. These systems appear to be less reactive to and threatened by the hospitalization of a member. In fact many such families tend to detach and withdraw from the member, who is "dumped off" at the hospital. We have even seen a situation in which a borderline family left for vacation immediately after leaving a member at the hospital.

Since this family typology is able to accommodate to a somewhat broader range of events and situations, their withdrawal from the member represents in part a temporary experience of relief from the intense involvement with this member prior to the hospitalization. It also may be viewed as a coping mechanism which delays a more reactive response to the separation. In other words, this type of borderline family has greater internal resources to allow a "scape-goated" member to be removed temporarily to restabilize the system.

However, these systems are often more difficult to maintain in community therapy. Their defensive perception is that by removing the identified member the system will remain calm and functional. Thus, the continuation of ongoing community therapy in the absence of the identified member may be experienced by the family not only as a nagging reminder of the role that person played in the system but also as an insidious threat to their reformulated status. The community therapist and the inpatient treatment team may have difficulty engaging the remainder of the family system to support or participate in treatment with the hospitalized member.

THE INTERFACE BETWEEN FAMILY AND HOSPITAL SYSTEMS

Jane stabilized fairly quickly within the structure of the hospital. After the initial 2 weeks of hospitalization, the inpatient team, frustrated by Bill's lack of involvement, negotiated a coordinated treatment plan that would utilize the community family therapist to supplement the ongoing inpatient therapeutic efforts. The inpatient team also continued to monitor Jane's medication. Interestingly, Bill agreed to participate in the family therapy at this point if it was held outside the hospital. The community therapist worked out an arrangement with the hospital team so that Jane could attend these sessions at the family therapist's office if Bill transported her to and from the hospital and as long as the inpatient team was satisfied that Jane's behavior did not indicate a suicidal risk.

Two sessions were conducted in the family therapist's office, the first with Bill and Jane, and the second with the parents and the two children. Unfortunately, it was during the second session that Bill announced that he could no longer pay the hospital costs and that he had already advised Jane's inpatient psychiatrist to arrange for her discharge the next day. This surprised the children as well as Jane, and unfortunately because of timing issues, this decision had not been communicated to the inpatient team or to this therapist. The efforts to deal with the impact of Bill's decision on both Jane and the children in this session were fruitless.

When hospitalization is indicated, the community therapist must be able to recognize the hospital as a therapeutic resource and system in and of itself. Each hospital has its own rules, structures, and hierarchies which the identified member and the family system must deal with. It is the hospital treatment team's responsibility to engage the family in an ongoing working relationship. If the hospital genuinely regards the family as a vital part of the overall treatment process, then it will not view family members as merely a source of information, financial responsiblity, or even harassment. It has been observed elsewhere that the more the hospital staff values their treatment program the more likely they are to initiate and establish working relations with the families of hospitalized members (Lansky, 1977).

If the hospital is committed to treating the entire family system, it will not be bound by traditional lines of organizational hierarchy. Thus treatment decisions are not unilaterally imposed upon the "patient" but are generated through the interaction among the hospital treatment team, the community therapist, and the family. Canevaro has reported: "The institution has to take care of the whole family group in the 'tempo' each family has, placing the family into a multi-family framework in which the therapeutic staff stops playing transferential substitution roles to become actual therapeutic chaperones to all the members in the family group" (1981, p. 376).

Broadly conceived, the goals of hospitalization with regard to the family system include alleviation of life-threatening behaviors and the restablilization of the identified member and the ongoing family process such that community therapy can be resumed and carried out safely and constructively. Clinically, this may involve either returning the member to his or her prior role in the system and maintaining the system's balance or attempting a more dramatic shift in the family structure by utilizing the hospital's protective environment to push for second order change.

The goal of building an alliance between the community therapist and the hospital treatment team remains crucial to both these goals. If the hospital staff and the community therapist are unable or unwilling to work with one another, it is likely that effective treatment for the borderline family will be sabotaged. We have seen too many instances in which families suffered from needless competition, lack of co-ordination, or fundamentally different treatment approaches between community and hospital therapists. We have observed that any of these factors will tend to heighten the sense of abandonment and rage within borderline families, resulting in a closing of the system's external boundaries and relative unavailablity to either set of therapists.

Thus it becomes a mutual responsibility of the hospital treatment team and the community therapist to build and maintain a good working relationship throughout the period of hospitalization. Of course, it behooves the community therapist who is treating borderline families to establish such relationships with hospital therapists long before a crisis and the need for back-up occurs.

From the perspective of the community therapist, particularly the seasoned family therapist, several clinical difficulties are inherent in the process of inpatient treatment. The foremost of these is that the hospitalization tends to solidify the relative skew in dynamics that occurs within the system when treatment focuses on one (hospitalized) member. The typical inpatient assessment and treatment regime, which may involve a 24-hour-a-day barrage of individual, group, and activity therapies, patient-staff team and community meetings, medical/pharmacological management, and monitored milieu interaction, often relegates family process and treatment to the background.

Studies have reported that the majority of psychiatric facilities attempt to offer at least verbal support for the involvement of the family in the treatment process (Anderson, 1977). In actuality, staff members often discourage involvement by being inaccessible to answer questions or to facilitate visits, by scheduling meetings at inconvenient times, by keeping the identified member sequestered from the family, or by believing that it was the family that victimized the hospitalized member.

From the community and family therapist's point of view, such policies and attitudes clearly fail to recognize that the power and continuing dynamics and loyalties of the family system will have great impact on the progress and outcome of inpatient treatment. Additionally, the more the community therapist is excluded from consultation regarding inpatient treatment, the more difficult it becomes to coordinate or sustain continuing therapy or even contact with the family. Thus by the time discharge from the hospitalization is announced, the "problem" or "bad" role of the hospitalized member has been solidified and reinforced within the system.

Readers should not be surprised that many inpatient therapists (Schween & Gralnick, 1969; Lansky, 1977; Anderson, 1977; Gunderson et al., 1980) have warned against offering family therapy in the initial days of hospitalization as potentially too upsetting to everyone involved, particularly if the identified member is acutely agitated or psychotic. However, as Boyd (1979) and Harbin (1979) have observed, such a strategy serves only to push family members to ignore pre-existing tensions and close ranks in a self-protective stance.

This relative dichotomy between community and family resources and inpatient treatment is evidenced particularly when home visits are planned for the hospitalized member. Such scheduled visits dramatize issues of the current family system's level of functioning without the hospitalized member, its potential for accommodating to the temporary re-entry of the identified member, and its potential for future community maintenance. Ideally, planning for this event should include the inpatient treatment team, the community family therapist, and the family and its identified member. Such an occasion can provide vital data for continuing assessment and therapy.

This stage in the treatment process should represent a clear transition to new accommodation by the family system and the initiation of a beginning transfer of treatment responsiblity to the community therapist. Each borderline family system will adjust differently to the re-entry of the identified family member: some will clearly regress and re-create former crises, others will pull together and deny former conflicts. The patterns will depend on such factors as timing, coordination between inpatient and community therapists, and the anticipation and management of other external and intergenerational influences. The inpatient and community management of whatever responses occur during the home visits will provide the basis for ongoing and hopefully coordinated therapy directed toward eventual discharge.

Similarly, potential collusive and reactive patterns on the part of the family will begin to emerge as the inpatient team announces a plan for discharge. Once again, the reactivity in the family system may range from regression to denial depending on the family typology and the system's relative preparation for either a renewal of homeostasis or potential reorganization. The therapists should not be surprised if new forms of conflict emerge at or shortly after discharge. Other crises may arise throughout the intergenerational system. A new identified, problematic member may emerge or a crisis in the marital relationship may erupt. The anxiety that the borderline system may experience in the face of losing the structure and support from the hospitalization may evoke previously undisclosed information about the identified member or other family members in an effort to delay or sabotage discharge.

It should be apparent that the drama of change will reverberate throughout the entire intergenerational borderline system whether or not issues of hospitalization and discharge are being addressed. It is our belief that the community therapist, working from a broad systemic view of borderline family behavior and in concert with an inpatient treatment team, can effectively assess and anticipate the need for hospitalization and the resultant therapeutic impact on the entire system.

Jane left the hospital the following day. The children were to remain with Bill's parents for several more days until Jane "got settled." The day after Jane returned home she picked up Sarah after school from the grandmother's house and took her to visit Jane's parents across town. That same afternoon John went to his home, found an extra set of keys to his father's car, walked to his father's office, drove the car away, and crashed it into a telephone pole across the street from his grandfather's office. The next appointment with the family therapist was still 3 days away . . . .

Chapter 6

Overview and Reflections

The intent of this work has been to present to the reader a cogent case for the role of systemic family therapy as the treatment of choice in the delivery of clinical services to borderline families. The effectiveness of developing family therapy strategies is based on a systemic clinical assessment of intergenerational etiological factors and interactional patterns which occur in borderline families. Thus, we have devoted a large portion of this work to reporting and describing the structural and process features that we have observed in borderline families. To further enhance our findings, we have reviewed the related psychiatric literature on the borderline condition and attempted to integrate these data with our observations into a systems model for assessment and treatment.

We have utilized intergenerational systemic family theory to organize the data and patterns that we believe support the designation of clinical borderline families. In presenting borderline family systems as a clinical family typology, we have introduced a variety of new systemically oriented concepts which we hope will assist the reader in understanding and recognizing the assessment features of the borderline family. Based on our observations of these systems' unique structures and interactional processes, we have also presented an overall model of family therapy which addresses the difficult clinical dynamics of working with borderline families.

125

Conducting therapy with borderline individuals and families remains one of the most challenging and difficult tasks for mental health practitioners. Throughout this work, we have considered the critical dimensions of the personal and professional roles of the therapist as they interface with the drama and often terror of the borderline system. We believe that it is important for the reader-as-therapist to track his or her own clinical experiences and struggles with borderline families in the issues that we have identified in this text. In clinical practice, the acquisition of new knowledge must always be integrated into one's personal therapeutic style before it can be operationalized effectively in applied skills.

This brief chapter will present an overview of the major issues, concepts, and strategies identified in this work. It will also provide an opportunity for reflections about our study and future work in this area.

THE ROLE OF THE THERAPIST

It has been our experience, and that of our associates and clinical students over the past decade, that family therapy provides more effective therapeutic control and containment with better therapeutic outcomes than similar work limited solely to individual therapy with an identified borderline individual. However, the therapist's work with the borderline family does not shield him or her from the drama, impulsivity, manipulation, and acting out associated with treating the borderline condition. In fact, this symptomatic reactivity that occurs throughout these family systems challenges the family therapist in areas of defining personal boundaries and clinical management. We have recommended that therapists consider the following guidelines in their treatment roles:

1. Beginning therapists should always work with or seek the supervision of a seasoned family therapist who can provide co-therapy or ongoing, weekly supervision.
2. Define personal and therapeutic boundaries firmly; be clear when you need to enter the system for

therapeutic gain and when you need to remain outside of the system to maintain therapeutic control.

3. Observe your own personal responses or reactivity to the family in treatment; be aware of your vulnerability to being pulled into these enmeshing systems as well as your tendency to withdraw in the face of manipulation and devaluation.

4. Maintain therapeutic control in order to manage the impulsivity and reactivity of the system.

5. Recognize the splitting and projective identification processes as systemic defenses that, at some point in the therapy, will be directed toward you as therapist.

6. Develop strategies to creatively engage and involve differing aspects of the family system which can be used to diffuse intensity and maintain therapeutic control.

7. Work closely with other allied professionals who are often involved with borderline families.

8. Develop a network of colleagues for consultation and friends for play so that you can maintain your own perspective on reality. Remember, you need all the help you can get!

ASSESSMENT FEATURES AND CONCEPTS

One of the most exciting aspects of this study occurred when the review of accumulated case data on identified borderline clients began to reveal similar patterns in family dynamics and structure. As we consulted with associates and refined our analyses, the consistency of patterns became striking. However, the more dramatic finding did not occur until several years into the study. It was after we had developed fairly clear concepts to define recognizable "borderline" family dynamics that we were able to confirm the presence of these identical dynamics within clinical families in which no borderline individual had been identified or diagnosed.

In some of these families a case could be made for one of the parent's displaying pre-clinical borderline traits. This was more typically a mother, and we designated this member of the family the "borderline carrier." However, it was not these symptoms, associated with this borderline carrier, that were identified as the presenting problem at the onset of therapy. More typically, it was the family's perception of threatening or terrorizing behavior displayed by one of the children. Less often the presenting problem was depression in one of the children. These clinical observations moved the impact of our study far beyond simply identifying the family dynamics of diagnosed borderline individuals. At this stage of the study, we had the basis for attempting to define the clinical typology of borderline families.

The following is a review of the major concepts arising from our study which provide the basis for defining and assessing the borderline family:

Family of Origin. The parents in the borderline family have almost always grown up in highly enmeshing family of origin systems. Occasionally, the non-borderline carrier represents a disengaging family of origin system (see the case example of Lenny in Chapter 3). Their own parents' emotional availability was limited usually because they had remained highly dependent on their own family of origin parents. Typically, a parent in the borderline carrier's family of origin displayed a chronicity of either serious mental or physical disabilities. This led to a child in this system, i.e., the future borderline carrier, being pulled into a highly parentified/caretaking role. The enmeshing qualities of this family of origin system made it difficult for the children to separate and leave home.

Mate Selection. In these systems, marriage often represented an escape to adulthood. The borderline carrier, whose parentified role had been reinforced over many years, selects a more passive/dependent mate who not only needs an adult caretaker but can tolerate the controlling aspects of this parentified partner (complementarity). Both spouses remain emotionally tied to their respective families of origin (vertical loyalties) and little emotional bonding occurs in their own relationship.

Splitting as a Systemic Defense in the Family. Positive and negative emotions, and even thoughts, which occur within the family's interactions become split apart from one another and experienced as separate entities by family members. This distorts the family's perception of reality such that events or persons become recognized as all "right" or "wrong" or "good" or "bad."

Projective Identification as a Systemic Defense in the Family. The qualities defining certain roles, e.g., "good" or "bad," are projected through the family's routine interactional process. These become internalized such that all family members play out rigidly defined role assignments within the system.

Coexisting Triangles. Borderline family systems display a somewhat unique structural pattern whereby two central triangles clearly exist simultaneously within the same system. Most families display one central triangle. These triangles serve to balance the functioning and stability of the system, and typically engage one child in each of the respective triangles.

The Omnipotent/Pseudo-Parentified Child. This child portrays the "good child" portion of the split within the family system. While they are pulled into the spousal subsystem and highly idealized (omnipotence), the borderline carrier's own intensely parentified role does not relinquish control of the actual caretaking duties (thus the child's pseudo-parentified role). This child acts without consequences and becomes highly manipulative.

The Persecuting Child. This is the "bad child" portion of the splitting process. Unlike a scapegoated child who more typically acts out away from the system, this child redirects the projected anger and conflict back onto the family through often threatening behaviors directed toward the family members. This allows the child to remain in the enmeshing system and contain the anger immediately outside the marital subsystem. It is this child who may often be identified as the presenting problem for therapy.

Family Themes/Myths. Themes and myths characterize most family systems. As certain perceptions or beliefs about reality, they are accepted by all family members and pervade the entire system. In clinical families they are often more prominent and rigid. The central themes/myths that we have observed in the borderline families are: 1. "negative feelings are destructive," and 2. "loss and separation are intolerable." The fear of negative feelings is an intergenerationally derived phenomenon and is reconfirmed by the family's display of intense conflict. The fear of separation and loss is also intergenerationally derived and serves to keep members tied, emotionally and physically, to the intergenerational system.

Structural Flexibility Characteristics of Borderline Systems. The organization and functioning of borderline systems appear to range across a continuum regarding the relative flexibility of their structural patterns. The more rigid the splitting, projection, boundaries, and role assignments within the system, the lower is their structural flexibility and thus the greater the difficulty to engage in therapy. Less rigid borderline systems display less social isolation, somewhat less intensity, and greater adaptation to external roles. Their structures are experienced as more flexible and they are somewhat easier to engage in therapy.

FAMILY THERAPY STRATEGIES

We hope by this stage of the text that the reader has gained an appreciation of family therapy as a very different way of understanding human behavior that involves the reciprocal patterns of interaction across a multigenerational system. One of our goals in this work, in addition to explicating our findings and furthering an understanding of the borderline family, was to demonstrate the viability and effectiveness of family therapy with this clearly recognized psychiatric dysfunction. We need to reiterate that conducting family therapy requires an epistemological shift away from the sole linear focus on individual dynamics and behavior to broadly conceptualizing the symptomatic display of dysfunctional behaviors within the interactive milieu of the intergenerational family system. The therapist cannot approach family therapy as simply another intervention or technique attached as a supplement to traditional individual psychotherapy.

The therapeutic goals and strategies that we have defined here for working with borderline families evolved out of our own backgrounds and experiences as family therapists, as well as from the pragmatic clinical struggles with these difficult cases. Some of the specific strategies represent typical family therapy interventions and are not unique specifically to borderline families. However, the broad cluster of goals and strategies that we have presented in Chapter 4 represents what we have found to be the most effective principles in working with borderline systems.

The specific goals of working with borderline families are discussed in Chapter 4 and are sumarized briefly here:

1. Decrease system patterns of splitting and enhance family members' ability to tolerate ambivalence.
2. Decrease projective identification interactions within the system, repair distortions, and restore individual members as "whole" persons.
3. Change the roles of the "good" child and the "bad" child, reduce rigidly defined role behavior, and allow more affiliative levels of interaction to emerge.
4. Reduce the family of origin loyalties of the parents by closing the external boundaries to protect and define the nuclear system.
5. Re-establish internal subsystem boundaries to reduce intergenerational intrusions and define an effective hierarchy.

These goals set the stage for the actual clinical strategies and interventions. The strategies that we have identified are linked directly to our working hypotheses and the clinical assessment features of the borderline system.

1. Developing and Maintaining a Therapeutic Structure. The most critical phase of conducting family therapy with borderline systems is at the beginning—the first telephone contact, defining the participants of the first interview, the first session. Defining a therapeutic structure establishes much-needed control for the therapist and in turn identifies the therapy setting and process as a "safe" place for the family to be. It is much more than establishing rapport or a simple alliance. The therapist must engage the family members while at the same time recognizing their defenses and respecting their boundaries. This early process always represents for the therapist a precarious balance between separation and connection to the system. Defining the therapuetic structure for a borderline family requires a more explict and direct approach than therapists typically employ with other cases. Specifically, it involves setting explicit rules governing time, participants, and safety. We have emphasized throughout the text the importance of maintaining therapeutic control with borderline families. Defining the structure from the beginning of the therapy process establishes control, which is necessary if the family is to continue in therapy.

2. Reality Testing with the Family. The therapist's representation of reality is a component of most forms of psychotherapy. We have found that it plays a crucial role in challenging and gradually correcting the perceptual and affective distortions common in borderline systems. This clinical role brings the therapist into direct contact with the primary system defenses of splitting and projective identification, as well as with the rigid role assignments and narrow range of affect. This therapeutic role emerges through the early phases of treatment and continues to the conclusion of the therapy process.

3. Interactional Disengagement. As we worked with borderline families, we recognized that the systemic procedure associated with reality testing involved what we have termed *interactional disengagement*. This involves clinical interventions designed to alter rigid role assignments by disengaging family members from the intensity of their interactions and projective identification patterns. The therapist intervenes to interrupt the projective loops, alter the reinforcing messages regarding prescripted roles, and introduce new information into the system. As with reality testing, this strategy is implemented throughout the therapy process.

4. Working with the Intergenerational System. We have identified the pervasiveness of intergenerational dynamics and influences throughout the borderline system. These powerful loyalties must be integrated into the therapy process. In some cases they may be introduced cognitively through the use of genograms and the exploration of family of origin data. However, it has been our experience that the actual involvement of family of origin members in the therapy process provides the greatest impact in challenging and attempting to redefine these prominent loyalties. As we have indicated, the involvement of family of origin members in the therapy process with borderline families can trigger primitive, and potentially destructive, emotions and should be planned only by experienced therapists.

5. Solidification of the Marital Alliance and Sibling Subsystem. At the stage of therapy where the intensity has been contained and some of the distortions have been removed, the therapist begins to identify and mark new boundaries which will serve to define and separate the marital subsystem from the sibling subsystem. This involves the restructuring of the system itself and can be accomplished only after progress has been made in detriangulating the good and bad children's roles and allowing some new marital interaction to emerge. Success in this process involves careful balancing by the therapist to allow family members to move out of their stereotyped roles. The success of this restructuring marks movement toward the final phase of therapy in which members are experienced as whole persons, subsystems are free of intrusions, and the reactivity triggered by the splitting and projective identification processes is diminished.

FUTURE DIRECTIONS

This work represents an effort to redefine, from a family systems perspective, a recognized psychiatric dysfunction by conceptualizing descriptive clinical data into a clinical model of assessment and treatment. From a strict research position, we are cognizant of the weaknesses of this type of study and tend to view it as a necessary first step in defining a clinical typology for further investigation. Within the emerging family therapy field, this juxtapositioning of theory and clinical data reflects both the deficits and the growing edges of the field.

In reflecting back over the course of this project, there are, of course, many unanswered questions, hunches, and even unspoken hypotheses that remain regarding the definition of borderline families. We list them here as stepping-stones for further inquiry.

Research Issues

Use inpatient and outpatient control groups to monitor structural changes in borderline systems.
Evolve better systemically and interactionally based instruments to provide more effective empirical definitions.

Conduct an in-depth, single-case designed study that would compare the internal family dynamics between a system with a diagnosed borderline mother and a system with an identified persecuting child.

Pursue the identification and measurement of further intergenerational data.

Conduct comparative clinical outcome studies utilizing a variety of family therapy approaches.

Analyze the before and after internal interactional and structural patterns of the family of a diagnosed borderline parent who reports successful completion of individual, psychodynamic treatment.

In a more empirical study, control for variables such as socioeconomics, race, and ethnicity.

The Role of the Therapist

Study therapists who have been burned out or sexually seduced by individual borderline clients.

Compare the personal resources of therapists who report ongoing success with borderline individuals or families.

Study the comparative subjective responses of individual and family therapists following ongoing clinical sessions with borderline dynamics.

How might the comparative styles of family therapists, (in the use of humor, confrontation, etc.) affect both management and outcome issues in treatment?

Clinical Issues

How do good and bad role assignments in childhood endure in adult relationships and life experiences?

What are the comparative adult adjustment patterns for the good and the bad children?

Study the fifth generation of borderline families, i.e., the children of the good and bad children, to determine the continuation, diffusion, or replacement of borderline patterns.

Look more carefully at families in which the borderline carrier is the father.

Investigate the specific family of origin variables and patterns in the etiology of diagnosed male borderline individuals.

Look more carefully at how the identified structural patterns vary in borderline families with only one child.

In borderline families with more than two children, examine how the non-triangulated children differ from the triangulated ones.

We hope that this text will be viewed as an open-ended work that will gain further relevance from the unique clinical experiences and resources of each reader as well as from much-needed future empirical assessment and outcome studies. At this point, we send the reader back to his or her ongoing clinical practice with borderline families with the hope that those families will benefit from any new perspectives or insights the reader has gained.

Glossary of Terms

Since this work addresses a broad range of practitioners and attempts to integrate, theoretically, a variety of resources and give definition to new concepts, the following glossary has been developed. Terms and concepts used in family therapy are defined and new concepts developed in the course of this study are introduced.*

Bad Child   A term utilized in family therapy to describe the child in the family on whom is projected traits perceived as incompetent, irresponsible, or destructive; occurs typically within the family system as a result of scapegoating; in the borderline family we have conceived the term persecuting child to describe the special characteristics of this child's role which occurs as a direct result of splitting within the system (see Good Child).

Balance   The process in family systems whereby various components, e.g., individuals, dyads, or subsystems, behave in a reciprocal and circular manner in order to maintain the system in a functional state and to ensure its survival; the clinical assessment of systemic balance must involve the intergenerational systems.

---

*Further descriptions of systemic family therapy terms may be found in the following references: American Association for Marriage and Family Therapy, 1984; Simon, Stierlin, and Wynne, 1985; and Nichols and Everett, 1986.

Borderline Carrier   A term conceived in this study based on our observation that borderline families may not have a single symptomatic individual who can be diagnosed as borderline; thus a family member, often the mother, may carry borderline traits from prior family of origin experiences even though they may not be displayed overtly. In borderline families the symptomatic individual may be an acting-out or depressive child or an adult with borderline characteristics. In family assessment one does not look solely for a "borderline individual" but at the broader dysfunctional constellation.

Borderline Family   A family typology conceived in this study which displays characteristic borderline dynamics and patterns, not simply in an individual, but operationalized and identifiable throughout the family system. The typical assessment traits of this system include patterns of splitting and projective identification involving typically two children in coexisting triangles.

Boundaries   An important clinical assessment concept in family therapy which identifies abstract markers between and among systems and subsystems. Boundaries define which family members are within or outside of a particular system, e.g., marital, parent-child. Boundaries can be characterized as rigid or flexible, diffuse, open, or closed. External boundaries define and mark the broad nuclear family system vis-a-vis intergenerational loyalties and family of origin ties and the social network; internal bondaries mark the relationships between the specific internal family subsystems, e.g., marital, sibling.

Centripetal/Centrifugal Patterns   Describes the process of adolescent separation according to differential family mechanisms (Stierlin, 1973) (see Fig. A–1); the centripetal family process binds members to the system and the adolescent feels too weak to separate; the centrifugal family process lacks internal cohesiveness and tends to expel the adolescent from the system early and forcefully. (See Disengaging System; Enmeshing System).

Coexisting Triangles   While most family systems have a central triangle that is the focus of power and/or balance for the entire system, very large systems or exceptionally unstable systems, e.g., the borderline family system, require at least two central triangles to maintain a balanced

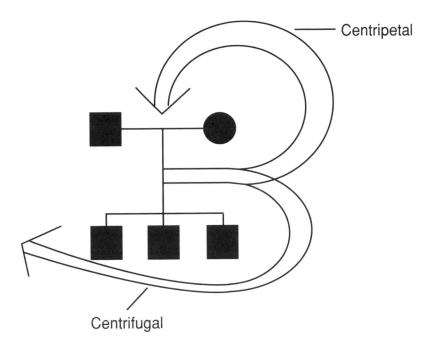

FIGURE A–1. Centripetal and Centrifugal Family Patterns

condition; as conceived in this study for clinical assessment the borderline family typically engages in a splitting and projective process in which the roles of the "good" and the "bad" children each serve as the focal point of one of the coexisting triangles.

Complementarity   In the assessment of marital dynamics this concept defines the underlying balance of a dyadic relationship in which reciprocal needs form the basis for attachment and bonding; typical patterns of complementarity may involve controlling-dependent or obsessive-hysterical roles, for example.

Disengaging System   A clinical assesssment concept from Minuchin's (1967, 1974) structural family therapy theory in which a family system's interactional and bonding patterns are characterized by distance, lack of interactional involvement, and typically rigid internal and diffuse external boundaries; individuals within these systems may gain greater degrees of independence but at the cost of interpersonal intimacy. (See *Enmeshing System.*)

Emotional Cut-off   A concept from Bowenian (1978) family therapy theory which describes the intergenerational process of dramatic emotional distancing or separation by an individual from the family of origin in order to attempt differentiation, such as moving 2000 miles away from the family of origin; occurs more typically in enmeshing systems.

Enmeshing System. The interactional and bonding patterns in a family system characterized by high levels of emotional attachment and/or reactivity with typically diffuse internal boundaries between individual and subsystems, and often rigid external boundaries (Minuchin, 1967, 1979). Individuals within these systems may be more comfortable with interpersonal closeness and intimacy but at the cost of differentiation and independence. (See *Disengaging System.*)

Family of Origin   The nuclear system in which an individual was born and reared, which is critical in clinical assessment for the identification of learned roles, behaviors, and loyalties; the biological family; may include lateral relatives, e.g., aunts, cousins, grandparents.

Family Myths/Themes   A descriptive concept in family therapy which identifies the intrinsic perceptions, present in most family systems, that define mutually perceived aspects of reality, often distorted. Myths/themes are shared typically by all members of the family system, e.g., paranoia, or a distrust of males. In the borderline family, myths/themes focus on the belief that "negative feelings are destructive" and "loss and separation are intolerable."

Feedback   A concept from cybernetic theory which describes a central dynamic in the life of all systems whereby events or behaviors loop back in a circular fashion to influence the original system or series of events; defines the difference in a systems orientation of understanding behavior from the traditional linear/mechanistic model which perceives event A as influencing event B, which in turn influences event C; explains how the family system as a unit accommodates to both internal and external influences which may produce a homeostatic rebalancing or push the system to new levels of interaction.

Genogram   A diagram useful in clinical assessment which depicts the various components of a family system across multiple generations, e.g, family members, relationship patterns, losses, and other life events. (See Fig. A–2.)

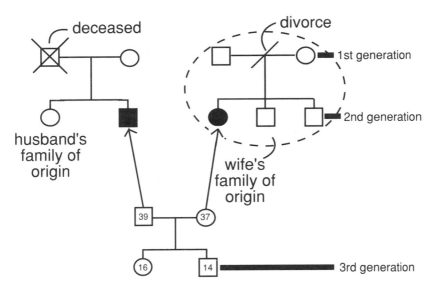

FIGURE A–2. A Three Generational Genogram

Good Child   A family therapy concept which identifies the child in a family on whom idealized, positive, and often powerful traits are projected; an example is the child who is assigned to take over parental and caretaking tasks (see *Parentification*); this study has identified the good child in the borderline family as the omnipotent/pseudo-parentified child; this role results from the systemic process of splitting and projection whereby this child becomes the focus of one of two co-existing triangles, and the bad child the focus of the other.

Loyalties   Defined in Boszormenyi-Nagy and Spark's (1973) intergenerational family therapy theory as the historical and present levels of emotional attachment and sense of personal responsibility which occur within relationships as well as to multiple generations of the family system. *Horizontal loyalties* describe the bonding that occurs in close peer relationships such as the marital relationship; *vertical loyalties* describe the ongoing feelings of attachment to and feelings of responsibility for one's own family of origin or to specific members throughout the intergenerational system.

Mate Selection   An interactional process that links both perceived and idealized personal characteristics of two individuals into a new dyadic system through the selection of a prospective mate; involves both conscious and unconscious dynamics; important in clinical assessment because it identifies aspects of each individual's present attraction and personal needs with significant past family of origin roles and relationship expectations which will define the newly formed interactive system.

Omnipotent/Pseudo-Parentified Child   A term conceived in this study to describe the unique characteristics of the parentified child within the borderline family. The typical assessment characteristics of the parentified child involve high degrees of manipulation within the system, acting without consequences, and yet becoming the focal point of balance for the system. All of these features are apparent in the borderline system yet, unlike the typical parentified child, this child is not allowed the power to perform a truly nurturing or caretaking role; that is usually reserved for the parental borderline carrier. This is the role of the *good child* (see) in one of the co-existing triangles. (See *Parentification.*)

Parentification   A concept from family therapy which describes the process whereby a child, or other family member, accepts through projection an excessive sense of responsibility for the functioning and well-being of the family or members within the family; for example, a child may actually take on excessive duties in the care of siblings or parents. The process functions to diffuse or divert stress from other interactional locations and may occur within a nuclear system or intergenerationally.

Persecuting Child   A term conceived in this study to describe special characteristics of a scapegoated child in the borderline family. A child accepts the projected anger from the family, and rather than simply acting this out through delinquent activities outside the family as would the typical scapegoat, this child turns the anger back onto the family in a persecuting and often terrorizing manner. This is the role of the *bad child* (see) in one of the co-existing triangles. (See *Scapegoating.*)

Process   In family therapy this term refers to the life and movement that occurs within a family system at a variety of levels, e.g., verbal and nonverbal interactive behavior, the system's accommodation to direct and meta-informational exchanges, homeostatic rebalancing. It may occur either in the system over time or in the system's or subsystem's current interaction.

Projective Identification   A psychodynamic concept that describes the interactive process whereby unacceptable or denied subjective aspects of an individual are projected onto another individual in a close relationship; the latter individual accepts the projection and begins to behave reciprocally according to the content of the projected data. Unlike simple projection in which the projected parts are left with the other person, here the projecting individual seeks to induce conformity in the behavior of the other person. In the borderline family, unacceptable dynamics regarding ambivalence, anger, and the fear of loss are projected collectively onto the individuals who become the *good child* (see) and the *bad child* (see) in the co-existing triangles. The children accept the projection and behave accordingly. In borderline family systems the projective data form the basis of the family's internal mythology.

Pseudo-Mutuality   A classic alignment and interactional defense, identified by Wynne and colleagues (1958), which covers and obscures underlying splits and conflicts within a family. The family members portray an image of fitting together while experiencing the potential of differentiation as a threat.

Scapegoating   The process whereby stress or conflict within a family system is accepted by a family member, typically a child, and acted out in often behaviorally disruptive or delinquent activities. This projective process serves to diffuse or divert stress away from the marital subsystem.

Splitting   A psychodynamic concept that describes a defensive process whereby an individual, unable to manage ambivalence in a relationship, separates the representations of an object into all "good" and all "bad" components. In the borderline family system the splitting process occurs collectively with the projection process; the collectively split good and bad traits are projected typically onto two children, i.e., the *good child* (see) and the *bad child* (see). (See *Projective Identification.*)

Structure   A family therapy concept that refers to the spatial arrangement of components or subsystems within a family, e.g., the sibling and parent-child subsystems. In clinical assessment this reflects the underlying organization of the system and may be either fixed or changing. (See *Process.*)

Structural Flexibility   A term conceived in this study to define a clinical typology to aid in the assessment of borderline families. Low structural flexibility defines rigid and closed intergenerational systems in which the exchange of external information is limited and thus the role of the therapist in joining or entering this system becomes problematic; high structural flexibility describes systems which display a greater range of interactive patterns and somewhat less intensity. The structural characteristics of borderline families may range along this continuum.

System   A concept derived from the physical sciences which describes a unit of reciprocally interactive elements whose activities impinge on one another. This defines the foundation of family systems theory in which the family is recognized as a system in which the various members and subsystems form an interactive or organic whole and in which the movement of one member influences the reciprocal movement and location of all other members and subsystems. Relatively open family systems process information freely and allow members to move in and out of the system; relatively closed family systems limit exchange and function within more rigid boundaries. Systems function in a "steady state" where homeostatic mechanisms lend balance for survival and adaptive mechanisms offer spontaneity and the potential for growth.

Three Generational Persecutory Loop   A term conceived in this study to describe a circular pattern across generations in borderline families in which anger or aggression that has been denied and not "owned" within either the family of origin or parental generations is projected onto a third generation child, typically the "bad" or persecuting child, and redirected, in the fashion of a cybernetic loop, back toward, rather than away from, the system. It serves the dual function of diffusing intergenerational anger and keeping the child closely bound to the enmeshing system.

Triangles   An assessment concept in family therapy (defined extensively by Bowen, 1978) which identifies interactional triadic patterns occurring in all family systems which form relational building blocks. These triadic patterns among family members function by both balancing interactive patterns and diffusing stress within a dyad when a third member is triangulated into the interaction, e.g., a child may be pulled into marital conflict. These patterns may serve dysfunctional roles by diffusing intimacy or communication in a dyad, breaching intergenerational boundaries, or rigidly binding an individual within a triadic relationship (see Fig. A-3).

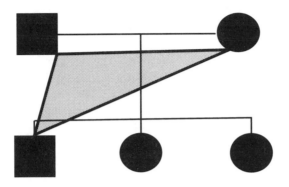

FIGURE A–3. Triangle Within a Nuclear Family System

References

Ackerman, N. W. (1958). *The psychodynamics of family life*. New York: Basic Books.

Adler, G. (1972). Helplessness in the helpers. *British Journal of Medical Psychology, 22*, 454–461.

Adler, G. (1979). The myth of the alliance with borderline patients. *Americal Journal of Psychiatry, 136*, 642–645.

Adler, G. (1980). A treatment framework for adult patients with borderline and narcissistic personality disorders. *Bulletin of the Menninger Clinic, 44*, 171–180.

American Association for Marriage and Family Therapy (1984). *Family therapy glossary*. Washington, D.C.: Author.

American Psychiatric Association (APA) (1980). *Diagnostic and statistical manual of mental disorders* (3rd ed.). Washington, D.C.: Author.

Americal Psychiatric Association (1987). *Diagnostic criteria from DSM-III-R*. Washington, D.C.: Author.

Anderson, C. M. (1977). Family intervention with severely disturbed inpatients. *Archives of General Psychiatry, 34*, 697–702.

Armelius, B., Kullgren, G., & Renberg, E. (1985). Borderline diagnosis from hospital records, reliability and validity of Gunderson's Diagnostic Interview for Borderlines (DIB). *Journal of Nervous and Mental Disorders, 173*, 32–34.

Beavers, W. R., & Voeller, M. N. (1983). Family models: Comparing and cointrasting the Olson circumplex model with the Beavers systems model. *Family Process, 22*, 85–97.

Blanck, R. & Blanck, G. (1974). *Ego psychology: theory and practice*. New York: Columbia University Press.

148   *References*

Boszormenyi-Nagy, I. & Spark, G. (1973). *Invisible loyalties.* New York: Harper & Row.

Bowen, M. (1965). Family psychotherapy with schizophrenia in the hospital and in private practice. In I. Boszormenyi-Nagy & J. L. Framo (Eds.), *Intensive family therapy.* New York: Harper & Row.

Bowen, M. (1971). Family therapy and family group therapy. In H. Kaplan & B. Sadock (Eds.), *Comprehensive group psychotherapy.* Baltimore: Williams & Wilkins.

Bowen, M. (1976). Family reactions to death. In P. J. Guerin (Ed.), *Family therapy: Theory and practice.* New York: Gardner Press.

Bowen, M. (1978). *Family therapy in clinical practice.* New York: Jason Aronson.

Bowlby, J. (1969). *Attachment and loss (Vol. I: Attachment).* New York: Basic Books.

Bowlby, J. (1973). *Attachment and loss (Vol. II: Separation).* New York: Basic Books.

Bowlby, J. (1980). *Attachment and loss (Vol. III: Loss: Sadness and depression).* New York: Basic Books.

Boyd, J. H. (1979). The interaction of family therapy and psychodynamic individual therapy in an inpatient setting. *Psychiatry, 42,* 99–111.

Bradley, S. J. (1981). The borderline diagnosis in children and adolescents. *Child Psychiatry and Human Development, 12,* 121–127.

Canevaro, A. (1981). Family therapy with psychotic patients: An institutional approach. *Journal of Marital and Family Therapy, 7,* 375–383.

Carter, L. & Rinsley, D. B. (1977). Vicissitudes of 'empathy' in a borderline adolescent. *International Review of Psychoanalysis, 4,* 317–325.

Chessick, R. D. (1972). Externalization and existential anguish in the borderline patient. *Archives of General Psychiatry, 27,* 764–770.

Dicks, H. (1967). *Marital tensions.* New York: Basic Books.

Eisenstein, V. (1951). Differential psychotherapy of borderline states. *The Psychiatric Quarterly, 25,* 379–401.

Fairbairn, W. R. D. (1952). *Psycho-analytic studies of the personality.* New York: Basic Books.

Fairbairn, W. R. D. (1954). *An object-relations theory of personality.* New York: Basic Books.

Fairbairn, W. R. D. (1963). Synopsis of an object-relations theory of personality. *International Journal of Psycho-Analysis, 44,* 224–225.

Fine, R. (1985). Countertransference reactions to the difficult patient. In H. Strean (Ed.), *Psychoanalytic approaches to the resistant and difficult patient.* New York: Haworth Press (pp. 7–45).

Finell, J. S. (1985). Projective identification: mystery and fragmentation. In H. Strean (Ed.), *Psychoanalytic approaches to the resistant and difficult patient.* New York: Haworth Press (pp. 47–62).

Fogarty, T. (1976). Triangles. *The family, 3,* 41–49.

Framo, J. L. (1972). *Family interaction: A dialogue between family researchers and family therapists.* New York: Springer.

Freud, A. (1965). *Normality and pathology in childhood.* New York: International Universities Press.

Grinker, R. R. & Werble, R. (1977). *The borderline patient.* New York: Jason Aronson.

Gunderson, J. G. & Singer, M. T. (1975). Defining borderline patients: an overview. *Americal Journal of Psychiatry, 132,* 1–10.

Gunderson J. G. & Kolb, J. E. (1978). Discriminating features of borderline patients. *Americal Journal of Psychiatry, 135,* 792–796.

Gunderson, G., Kerr, J., & England, D. W. (1980). The families of borderlines: A comparative study. *Archives of General Psychiatry, 37,* 27–33.

Gunderson, G., Kolb, J., & Austin, V. (1981). The diagnostic inter view for borderline patients. *American Journal of Psychiatry, 138,* 896–903.

Guntrip, H. (1967). The object-relations theory of W. R. D. Fairbairn. *American Handbook of Psychiatry, 3,* Ch. 17.

Guntrip, H. (1968). *Schizoid phenomena, object relations and the self.* New York: International Universities Press.

Guntrip, H. (1971). *Psychoanalytic theory, therapy, and the self.* New York: Basic Books.

Harbin, H. T. (1979). A family-oriented psychiatric inpatient unit. *Family Process, 18,* 281–291.

Hartmann, H. (1950). Comments on the psychoanalytic theory of the ego. *Psychoanalytic Study of the Child, 5,* 74–96.

Jacobson, E. (1964). *The self and the object world.* New York: International Universities Press.

Kernberg, O. F. (1968). The treatment of patients with borderline personality organization. *International Journal of Psychoanalysis, 49,* 600–619.

Kernberg, O. F. (1972). Early ego integration and object relations. *Annals of the New York Academy of Science, 193,* 233–247.

Kernberg, O. F. (1975). *Borderline conditions and pathological narcissism.* New York: Jason Aronson.

Kernberg, O. F. (1976). *Object relations theory and clinical psychoanalysis.* New York: Jason Aronson.

Kernberg, O. F. (1977). Structural change and its impediments. In P. Hartocollis (Ed.), *Borderline personality disorders*. New York: International Universities Press.

Klein, M. (1932). *The Psychoanalysis of children*. London: Hogarth Press.

Klein, M. (1946). Notes on some schizoid mechanisms. *International Journal of Psycho-analysis, 27*, 99–110.

Lansky, M. R. (1977). Establishing a family-oriented inpatient unit. *Journal of Operational Psychiatry, 8*, 66–74.

Mahler, M. S. (1971). A study of the separation-individuation process and its possible application to borderline phenomena in the psychoanalytic situation. *Psychoanalytic Study of the Child, 26*, 403–424.

Mahler, M., Pine, F., & Bergman, A. (1975). *The psychological birth of the human infant*. New York: Basic Books.

Malin, A. & Grotstein, J. S. (1966). Projective identification in the therapeutic process. *International Journal of Psycho-analysis, 47*, 26–31.

Maltsberger, J. T. & Buie, D. H. (1972). Countertransference hate in the treatment of suicidal patients. *Archives of General Psychiatry, 30*, 625–633.

Mandelbaum, A. (1977). Family treatment of the borderline patient. In P. Hartocollis (Ed.), *Borderline personality disorders*. New York: International Universities Press.

Mandelbaum, A. (1980). Family characteristics of patients with borderline and narcissistic disorders. *Bulletin of Menninger Clinic, 44*, 201–211.

Masterson, J. F. (1972). *Treatment of the borderline adolescent: A developmental approach*. New York: John Wiley & Sons.

Masterson, J. F. (1976). *Psychotherapy of the borderline adult*. New York: Brunner/Mazel.

Masterson, J. F. (1981). *The narcissistic and borderline disorders: An integrated developmental approach*. New York: Brunner/Mazel.

Masterson, J. F. (1983). *Countertransference and psychotherapeutic technique: Teaching seminars on psychotherapy of the border-line adult*. New York: Brunner/Mazel.

Masterson, J. F. & Rinsley, D. (1975). The borderline syndrome: The role of the mother in the genesis and psychic structure of the borderline personality. *International Journal of Psycho-analysis, 56*, 163–177.

Meissner, W. W. (1978). Theoretical assumptions of concepts of the borderline personality. *Journal of the American Psychoanalytic Association, 26*, 559–598.

Meissner, W. W. (1983). Notes on the levels of differentiation within borderline conditions. *Psychoanalytic Review, 70*, 179–209.

Mendez, A. M. & Fine, H. J. (1976). A short history of the British school of object relations and ego psychology. *Bulletin of the Menninger Clinic*, 40, 37–382.

Minuchin, S., Montalvo, B. G., Guerney, B., Rosman, B. L., & Schumer, F. (1967). *Families of the slums: An exploration of their structure and treatment.* New York: Basic Books.

Minuchin, S. (1974). *Families and family therapy.* Cambridge: Harvard University Press.

Minuchin, S. & Fishman, H. C. (1981). *Family therapy techniques.* Cambridge: Harvard University Press.

Nadelson, T. (1976). Victim, victimizer: Interaction in the psychotherapy of borderline patients. *International Journal of Psychoanalytic Psychotherapy*, 5, 115–129.

Nichols, W. C. & Everett, C. A. (1986). *Systemic family therapy: An integrative approach.* New York: Guilford.

Oberndorf, C. P. (1948). Failures with psychoanalytic therapy. In P. Hoch (Ed.), *Failures in psychiatric treatment.* New York: Grune & Stratton.

Perry, J. C. & Klerman, G. L. (1978). The borderline patient: A comparative analysis of four sets of diagnostic criteria. *Archives of General Psychiatry*, 35, 141–150.

Rinsley, D. B. (1978). Borderline psychopathology: A review of etiology, dynamics and treatment. *Psycho-Analysis*, 5, 45–53.

Ritvo, S. (1975). Some relationships of the rapprochement subphase of infantile and adult neurosis. *Journal of Philadelphia Association of Psychoanalysis*, 2, 97–103.

Robbins, M. O. (1976). Borderline personality organization: The need for a new theory. *Journal of the American Association*, 24, 831–853.

Rosner, S. (1969). Problems of working through with borderline patients. *Psychotherapy: Theory, Research, and Practice*, 6, 43–45.

Schween, P. A. & Gralnick, A. (1969). Factors affecting family therapy in the hospital setting. *Comprehensive Psychiatry*, 7, 424–431.

Searles, H. F. (1986). *My work with borderline patients.* New Jersey: Jason Aronson.

Settlage, C. (1975). On the aggressive aspect of early psychic development and the genesis of the infantile neurosis. *Journal of the Philadelphia Association of Psychoanalysis*, 2, 97–103.

Shapiro, E. R. (1978). The psychodynamics and developmental psychology of the borderline patient: A review of the literature. *American Journal of Psychiatry*, 135, 1305–1314.

Shapiro, E. R., Zinner, J., Shapiro, R. L., & Berkowitz, D. A. (1975). The influence of family experience on borderline personality development. *International Review of Psycho-Analysis*, 2, 399–410.

Simon, F. B., Stierlin, H., & Wynne, L. C. (1985). *The language of family therapy: A systemic vocabulary and sourcebook.* New York: Family Process Press.

Singer, M. (1975). The borderline delinquent: The interlocking of intrapsychic and interactional determinants. *International Review of Psycho-Analysis, 2,* 429–437.

Skynner, R. (1981). *Systems of family and marital psychotherapy.* New York: Brunner/Mazel.

Slipp, S. (1980). Marital therapy for borderline personality disorders. *American Journal of Family Therapy, 8,* 67–70.

Stierlin, H. (1973). A family perspective on adolescent runaways. *Archives of General Psychiatry, 29,* 56–62.

Vogel, E. & Bell, N. W. (1960). The emotionally disturbed child as a family scapegoat. In N. W. Bell & E. Vogel (Eds.), *The family.* Glencoe, IL: Free Press.

Weldinger, R. J. & Gunderson, J. G. (1987). *Effective psychotherapy with borderline patients: Case studies.* New York: Macmillan.

Walsh, F. (1977). Family study 1976: 14 borderline cases. In R. Grinker & B. Werble (Eds.), *The borderline patient.* New York: Jason Aronson.

Williamson, D. S. (1981). Personal authority via termination of the intergenerational hierarchical boundary: A "new" stage in the family life cycle. *Journal of Marital and Family Therapy, 7,* 441–452.

Williamson, D. S. (1982a). Personal authority via termination of the intergenerational hierarchical boundary: II. The consultation process and the therapeutic method. *Journal of Marital and Family Therapy, 8,* 23–37.

Williamson, D. S. (1982b). Personal authority in family experience via termination of the intergenerational hierarchical boundary: III. Personal authority defined, and the power of play in the change process. *Journal of Marital and Family Therapy, 8,* 309–323.

Winch, R., Ktsanes, T., & Ktsanes, V. (1954). The theory of complementary needs in mate selection: An analytic and descriptive study. *American Sociological Review, 19,* 241–249.

Winnicott, D. W. (1960). The theory of parent-infant relationships. *International Journal of Psycho-Analysis, 41,* 585–595.

Winnicott, D. W. (1965). *The maturational processes and the facilitating environment.* New York: International Universities Press.

Winnicott, D. W. (1971). *Playing and reality.* London: Tavistock.

Wolberg, A. (1952). The 'borderline patient.' *American Journal of Psychotherapy, 6,* 694–701.

Wolberg, A. (1982). *Psychoanalytic psychotherapy of the borderline patient.* New York: Thieme-Stratton.

Wynne, L., Ryckoff, I. M., & Hirsch, S. I. (1958). Pseudomutuality in the family relations of schizophrenics. *Psychiatry, 21,* 205–220.

Zetzel, E. (1971). A developmental approach to the borderline patient. *American Journal of Psychiatry, 128,* 867–871.

Zinner, J. & Shapiro, E. R. (1972). Splitting in families of borderline adolescents. In J. Mack (Ed.), *Borderline states in psychiatry.* New York: Grune & Stratton.

Zuk, G. H. (1981). *Family therapy: A triadic-based approach.* New York: Human Sciences Press.

INDEX